green | designed

Christine Anna Bierhals

Fashion

PRÊT-À-PORTER . HAUTE COUTURE . STREET WEAR . CASUAL

avedition

„Ich glaube daran, dass Mode schön sein kann – von außen und auch von innen!" (Peter Ingwersen, Gründer und Chefdesigner von Noir).

Eine neue grüne Welle rollt auf uns zu. Aus dem Öko-Trend ist eine Lifestyle-Bewegung geworden, die die gesamte westliche Welt erfasst hat. Sie richtet sich gegen allzu rasante wirtschaftliche Entwicklungen und die damit einhergehende Massenproduktion. Gerade in der Welt der Mode findet derzeit eine grüne Revolution statt. Die Missstände in der Modeindustrie, die von Ausbeutung und Diskriminierung über Umweltverschmutzung bis hin zu verheerenden Ökobilanzen durch den Baumwollanbau reichen, werden immer offensichtlicher. Öko-Mode

hingegen wird ethisch korrekt produziert, hält weltweite Sozialstandards wie limitierte Arbeitszeiten oder Mindestlöhne ein, verzichtet auf Kinderarbeit, fördert den Anbau ökologischer Baumwolle und die Umstellung auf umweltfreundlichere Materialien und Farbstoffe oder recycelt alte Materialien zu neuen, modischen Kunstwerken. Sie ist gesund, nachhaltig und fair. Mode soll nicht mehr nur ein gutes Gefühl, sondern auch ein gutes Gewissen verschaffen.

Öko-Mode reflektiert einen natürlichen Wertewandel. Sie wird einem wachsenden Bedürfnis nach einem individuellen Lebensstil auf Basis von Gesundheit und Nachhaltigkeit gerecht. Für immer mehr Verbraucher spielt Umweltbewusstsein

eine ebenso große Rolle wie Qualitäts- und Modebewusstsein. Die so genannten „Neo-Ökos" verlangen nach ethisch und sozial einwandfreien Produkten mit Zertifikat und Biosiegel, die auf moderne Ästhetik und Stil nicht verzichten.

„green designed fashion" liefert einen Einblick in diesen neuen, grünen Lifestyle, der die ehemals unvereinbaren Aspekte Öko und Modernität miteinander verbindet. Die hier gezeigten Designer beweisen, dass Kleidung, die umwelt- und sozialverträglich entstanden ist, cool und modern sein kann. Heute erinnern die zeitgemäßen Kollektionen weder an die Ökobewegung der Hippies noch die der Yuppies der 80iger Jahre. Denn bei der Herstellung von Kleidung ist tech-

nisch inzwischen so viel möglich, dass Öko nicht mehr nach dem typischen Öko-Klischee aussieht. Das Buch zeigt die Bandbreite ethischer Mode, von der kleinen, originellen T-Shirt-Kollektion bis hin zu exklusiven Haute-Couture Modellen. Die innovativen Modefirmen, Charityprojekte und gemeinnützigen Organisationen vereinen die Begriffe Fair-Trade und Entwicklungshilfe mit Design und Individualität. Viele der hier gezeigten Designer können aufgrund hoher Material- und Lohnkosten noch nicht 100%ig die Kriterien einer ökologischen und sozial gerechten Produktion erfüllen. Trotzdem tragen sie alle dazu bei, ein ökologisches Bewusstsein zu schaffen.

„green designed fashion" honoriert dieses Bemühen. Denn abgesehen von mancher Kritik, Öko-Mode sei zu teuer, nur für Hedonisten oder verbessere das Firmenimage, ist doch jeder Versuch, ökologisch bewusst zu handeln, wirksam. Er stößt eine breite Masse oder kleine Zielgruppe auf die Wichtigkeit von Öko-Mode. Durch deren Bewusstseinswandel wird der ganze Markt dazu aufgefordert, sich dem Thema mehr und mehr zu widmen. Das Bemühen der Öko-Designer hat sich ausgezahlt und kommt auch an. Immer mehr moderne Öko-Messen, Verbände und Magazine deuten auf eine steigende Nachfrage hin. Dem ökologischen Bewusstseinswandel folgen viele neue Informationen und Begriffe, die bei den Verbrauchern für Verwirrung sorgen. Das

Buch bietet am Ende mit seinem Glossar einen kleinen Überblick über neues, ökospezifisches Vokabular, das in Zukunft bald alltäglich sein wird. Lernen Sie die neue Sprache und lassen Sie sich von ihr begeistern, denn die grüne Revolution ist mehr als eine Trenderscheinung! Einen Gegentrend zu dem Streben nach mehr Ökologie und Fairness wird es wohl kaum geben. Mehr Verschmutzung, mehr Korruption, mehr Kinderarbeit sind keine Alternative. Die grüne Welle rollt unaufhaltsam weiter.

Christine Anna Bierhals

"I believe that fashion can be beautiful—both on the outside and the inside!" (Peter Ingwersen, founder and chief designer of Noir).

A new green wave is rolling towards us. What used to be an eco trend, has become a lifestyle movement which is sweeping across the whole western world. It goes against lightning-fast economic development and the associated mass production. Especially the world of fashion is experiencing a green revolution. Injustices in the fashion industry which range from exploitation and discrimination right through to the disastrous ecological imbalance exemplified by cotton farming, are becoming more and more obvious. Eco fashion, on the other hand, is produced in an ethically correct way. It adheres to world-wide social standards such as limited working hours or minimum wages, manages without child labor, supports organic cotton farming, and the changeover to more environmentally friendly materials and dyes. It also recycles old materials to create new, fashionable pieces of art. It is healthy, sustainable, and fair. Fashion should not only induce a good feeling, but also a clear conscience.

Eco fashion reflects a natural change of values. It is determined by the growing need for an individual lifestyle based on health and sustainability. An ever growing number of consumers looks out for ecological awareness as much as for quality and design. The so-called "neo ecos" demand certified ethical and socially responsible products which have been awarded an eco accolade and display both modern aesthetics and style.

"green designed fashion" provides an insight into this new green lifestyle which for the first time combines the once opposing fields of eco and fashion. The designers presented in this book prove that ecological and socially correct apparel can be cool and modern. These days contemporary collections are nothing like the hippie eco trend nor the yuppie style of the 80s. This is because apparel manufacturing is technologically so advanced that eco is free of the typical eco cliché. This book shows the

possibilities of ethical fashion, ranging from small, original T-shirt collections right through to exclusive haute-couture. Innovative fashion firms, charity projects, and charitable organizations interlink fair trade and development aid with design and individuality. Because of the high costs for both materials and labor, many of the presented designers are not able to fulfill the criteria for ecological and socially responsible production to 100 percent. Nevertheless, they all contribute to raising ecological awareness.

"green designed fashion" honors their endeavors. Despite criticism that eco fashion is too expensive, for hedonists only, or simply tries to improve the company's image, every attempt of acting ecologically is a step in the right direction, as small target groups, if not the masses, take note of the importance of eco fashion. It is this change of attitude that can command a whole market to engage in the eco trend. The efforts of eco designers have paid off – they are becoming more and more popular. Increasing numbers of modern eco trade fairs, groups, and magazines indicate greater demand. With this new ecological awareness comes new information and terminology, both of which tend to confuse consumers. At the end of this book you will find a glossary which explains the basics of the new eco specific vocabulary – something which will be common knowledge in the near future. Learn the new language now and feel inspired by it, because the green revolution is more than just a trend. It is difficult to see an opposing movement to ecology and fairness—after all, do we have a choice? More pollution, more child labor, more corruption? This is no alternative for our planet. The green wave rolls on.

Christine Anna Bierhals

Amana Collection | Designers: Erin Tabrar (left), Helen Wood (right)

Fall Winter 2008/09

www.amana-collection.com

The English label Amana was brought to life in 2007 by designers Helen Wood and Erin Tabrar. The designer duo has been working with eco materials ever since. It is their aim to combine attractive designs with ethically sound production methods. Every piece of clothing is hand-crafted by seamstresses in Ain Leuh, a small village in the central Atlas mountains in Morocco. Amana uses pure, SKAL certified organic cotton, organic silk, and high-quality hemp mixed with bamboo, tencel, and soy for its collections. Amana believes that socially sound and sustainable actions are both prerequisite for, and form the basis of, long term partnerships with production firms. This entails good working conditions, prepayment, and provision of technical help and training. They voluntarily comply with IFAT guidelines (International Fair Trade Association). Amana focuses on trust, which also happens to be the translation of its Moroccan Arabic name.

Das englische Label Amana wurde 2007 von den Designerinnen Helen Wood und Erin Tabrar gegründet. Seitdem entwirft das Designer-Duo Mode aus Bio-Materialen. Ihr Bestreben ist es zudem, schönes Design mit ethisch gerechter Produktion zu vereinen. So wird jedes Kleidungsstück von Näherinnen in Ain Leuh, einem kleinen Dorf im Mittleren Atlas-Gebirge Marokkos handgefertigt. Amana verwendet für die Kollektionen durch Skal zertifizierte, reine, organische Baumwolle, organische Seide und hochwertigen Hanf gemischt mit Bambus, Tencel und Soja. Sozial gerechtes und nachhaltiges Handeln sieht Amana als Grundlage und Voraussetzung für langfristige Partnerschaften mit den Produktionsfirmen. Dazu gehören gute Arbeitsbedingungen, Vorauszahlungen und die Bereitstellung technischer Hilfe und Ausbildung. Auf freiwilliger Basis richten sich die Designerinnen nach den IFAT-Richtlinien (International Fair Trade Association). Amana setzt auf Vertrauen, was zugleich auch die Übersetzung ihres marokkanisch-, arabischsprachigen Labels ist.

AOI | Designer: Tatsuki Takino

Spring Summer 2007 (page 11), Fall Winter 2006/07 (page 12-13)
www.inspiri.eu

AOI produces luxurious and innovative fashion. It is not made, however, from opulent, newly produced materials, but from recycled goods. Old, hand-made silk kimonos form the basis of the collection. The designer Tatsuki Takino, half French, half Japanese, has been realizing his ideas since 2003. With his friend Romain Massau, he founded the AOI label in September 2005 and focused on the environmentally friendly recycling of materials. They collected old kimonos and transformed them into wearable pieces of art with new cuts and production processes. AOI combines traditional Asian kimono history with modern design. Each item is unique and tells a story, which is continued by its new wearer. Manual work and the use of recycled materials make each AOI creation something that is both very special and an example of socially responsible and environmentally friendly production processes.

AOI produziert luxuriöse und innovative Mode, die nicht aus opulenten, neu produzierten, sondern recycelten Materialien besteht. Grundlage für die Kollektion sind alte, handgemachte Seidenkimonos. Seit 2003 realisiert der Designer Tatsuki Takino, der halb Franzose, halb Japaner ist, seine Ideen mit eigenen Händen. Mit seinem guten Freund Romain Massau gründete er im September 2005 das Label AOI. Die Designer setzen hierbei auf umweltfreundliche „Wiederverwertung". Sie nutzen alte Kimonos als Rohstoff und transformieren sie mit modernen Schnitten und Verarbeitungsmethoden zu neuen, tragbaren Kunstwerken. AOI verbindet die traditionelle, asiatische Geschichte des Kimonos mit modernem Design. Jedes Kollektionsteil ist einzigartig und erzählt eine Geschichte, die in seinem neuen Träger eine Fortsetzung findet. Der Einsatz von Handarbeit und wiederverwerteter Materialien macht jede Kreation von AOI zum individuellen Schmuckstück und gleichzeitig zu einem Vorbild sozial gerechter und umweltfreundlicher Produktion.

Article 23 | Designer: Naia Rico

Fall Winter 2008/09
www.article-23.com

"Everyone who works has the right to just and favorable remuneration ensuring for himself and his family an existence worthy of human dignity, and supplemented, if necessary, by other means of social protection." The philosophy of this aptly named label is that of article 23 of the Universal Declaration of Human Rights. Article 23 sees itself as an ethically correct fashion label that respects the dignity of the individual. Designer and activist Naia Rico, who attended the renowned fashion schools of Central St. Martins and the London College of Fashion, presents modern everyday clothing that is both sophisticated and sporty. "Ethical, organic, and fashionable" are Article 23's buzzwords. The label combines both ecological and social awareness with trendy design and is thus proof that creativity and success do not preclude fair trade and sustainable development. Article 23 has moved production to a center in the slums of Bombay in India that supports self-employed seamstresses. The designer uses organic materials such as top quality eco cotton, silk or satin. In 2007, the label started collaborating with Conserve, an Indian charitable organization that makes accessories for Article 23 produced from recycled plastic bags.

„Jeder, der arbeitet, hat das Recht auf gerechte und befriedigende Entlohnung, die ihm und seiner Familie eine der menschlichen Würde entsprechende Existenz sichert, gegebenenfalls ergänzt durch andere soziale Schutzmaßnahmen." Auf den Artikel 23 der Allgemeinen Erklärung der Menschenrechte bezieht sich die Philosophie des gleichnamigen Lables. Article 23 sieht sich als ethisch korrektes Modelabel, das die Menschenwürde respektiert. Die Designerin und Aktivistin Naia Rico, die die renommierten Modeschulen Central St. Martins und das College of Fashion in London abschloss, präsentiert heute moderne Alltagskleidung, die „sophisticated" und sportiv zugleich ist. „Ethisch, organisch und modisch", so lauten die Schlagworte von Article 23. Das Label vereint ein ökologisches und soziales Bewusstsein mit trendigem Design und ist somit ein Beweis dafür, das Kreativität und Erfolg Fair-Trade und eine nachhaltige Entwicklung nicht ausschließen. Article 23 lässt seine Kollektionen in einem Zentrum, in dem selbstständige Näherinnen gefördert werden, in den Slums von Bombay in Indien fertigen. Die Designerin verwendet rein organische Materialien wie beste Bio-Baumwolle, Seide oder Satin. Zudem arbeitet das Label seit 2007 mit der gemeinnützigen, indischen Organisation „Conserve", die für das Label Accessoires aus recycelten Plastiktaschen produziert, zusammen.

Boat People | Designer: Elisabeth Prantner

Cocktail Dress made from 15 baby pants

www.lisad.com

The Berlin based Austrian Elisabeth Prantner is an artist and autodidact in the area of fashion design. Social criticism and ethics play major roles in her "Boat People," "Lisa D." and "Global Concern" labels. As a fashion artist, she incorporates socio-critical issues in her collections. Natural materials and local production in her Berlin studio are features of her environmentally friendly design philosophy. In her five limited series for Global Concern she rebels against epidemics, famine, child labor, war, and the repression of minorities. Elisabeth Prantner's design is therefore "green" in terms of ethical awareness and responsibility. She expresses her political and social commitment through her fashion.

Die in Berlin lebende Österreicherin Elisabeth Prantner ist Künstlerin und Autodidaktin im Bereich Modedesign. Gesellschaftskritik und Ethik spielen in ihren drei Linien „Boat People", „Lisa D." und „Global Concern" eine wichtige Rolle. Sozialkritische Themen verarbeitet sie in ihren Kollektionen als Modekünstlerin. Natürliche Materialien und die Produktion in ihrem Berliner Studio sind Merkmale ihrer umweltbewussten Design-Philosophie. In ihren fünf limitierten Serien für „Global Concern" lehnt sie sich gegen Epidemien, Hungersnöte, Kinderarbeit, Krieg und Unterdrückung von Minderheiten auf. Das Design von Elisabeth Prantner ist somit „Grün" im Sinne von ethischem Bewusstsein und Verantwortung. Ihr politisches und soziales Engagement trägt sie über ihre Mode nach außen.

Camilla Norrback

Fall Winter 2008/09

www.camillanorrback.com

The Swedish designer Camilla Norrback understands the term "eco-luxury" to mean ecological awareness and sustainability combined with luscious materials, high quality, and extraordinary design – something she has put into practice with her own fashion label in Stockholm since 1999. She almost exclusively uses environmentally friendly produced materials such as eco wool and cotton. Camilla Norrback is of the opinion that it is easy enough these days to produce ecologically sound fashion and that the designer is in no way hampered by his/her decision to go green. After all, even polyester can be produced using environmentally friendly processes. 2008 sees a new line using recycled polyester. Camilla Norrback's collections can be bought throughout Europe as well as the USA, Russia, Japan, and South Korea.

Der Begriff „Ecoluxury" bedeutet für die schwedische Designerin Camilla Norrback ökologisches Bewusstsein und Nachhaltigkeit, kombiniert mit üppigen Materialien, hochwertiger Qualität und außergewöhnlichem Design. Seit 1999 realisiert sie dies mit ihrem eigenen Modelabel in Stockholm. In ihren Kollektionen versucht sie, vor allem umweltfreundlich produzierte Stoffe, wie z.B. ökologische Wolle und Baumwolle, zu verwenden. Camilla Norrback vertritt die Meinung, dass es heutzutage ausreichend Möglichkeiten gibt, ökologisch gerechte Mode produzieren zu können. Dabei werden dem Design keinerlei künstlerische Grenzen gesetzt, denn sogar für Polyester gibt es mittlerweile umweltfreundliche Herstellungsprozesse. 2008 präsentiert die Designerin erstmals eine Linie, in der sie recyceltes Polyester verarbeitet. Die Kollektionen von Camilla Norrback sind in etlichen europäischen Ländern sowie in den USA, Russland, Japan und Korea zu finden.

Ciel | Designer: Sarah Ratty

Fall Winter 2008/09
www.ciel.ltd.uk

Ciel, the label by English fashion designer Sarah Ratty, counts as a pioneer of eco fashion. Her "hip", luxurious, and unique designs are based on an ecological philosophy, which she has acted on and lived since 1990 – her ethical and ecologically minded management is a case in point as reflected by her collaboration with "Labour Behind The Label" — an organization which fights for humane working conditions. Ciel uses organic cotton certified by "Control Union" and "GOTS", the "Global Organic Textile Standard", in all its cotton collections from lingerie to mainline womenswear collection. Embroidery is done by needlewomen employed on a fair trade basis. Materials consist of eco cotton, linen and wool, cupro silk, and hemp. All collections are produced from 80%–90% natural, sustainable, and ecological fabrics. Ciel pursues its goal to produce 100% ecologically, a fact that is supported by the "Oeco-Tex" and "Confidence in Textiles" certification of most of the materials it uses.

Ciel, das englische Modelabel der Designerin Sarah Ratty, gilt als Pionier im Bereich der Ökomode. Hinter dem „hippen", luxuriösen und besonderen Design steht eine starke Öko-Philosophie, die sich seit 1990 konsequent durchsetzt. Das zeigt sich vor allem in einer ethisch gerechten und ökologisch bewussten Unternehmensführung. Beispielhaft ist unter anderem die Zusammenarbeit mit „Labour Behind The Label", einer Organisation die sich für gerechte Arbeitsbedingungen einsetzt. Zudem verwendet Ciel organische Baumwolle, die von „Control Union" und „GOTS", dem „Global Organic Textile Standard" zertifiziert wurde. Stickereien werden auf Fair-Trade Basis von Handwerkerinnen angefertigt. Die Stoffe sind aus Bio-Baumwolle, Leinen und Wolle, Cupro Seide und Hanf. Alle Kollektionen sind zu 80%-90% aus natürlichen, nachhaltigen und ökologischen Stoffen gefertigt. Das Ziel, 100% ökologisch zu produzieren, verfolgt Ciel konsequent. Der Beweis: Die Materialien besitzen zum größten Teil das „Öko-Tex" und „Confidence in Textiles" Zertifikat.

Emily Katz

Fall Winter 2008/09
www.emilykatz.com

Designer Emily Katz launched her first women´s line in 2003. The collections are unique creations made by hand, dyed by hand and embroidered by hand. The designer focuses on timeless and classic designs that do not go out of fashion as well as on clothing that is easy on the conscience. This label from Portland, Oregon, presents small but politically correct collections of draped apparel made from sustainable and innovative materials such as water resistant fleece. Fabrics made of soy-jersey, hemp, recycled denim, and eco cotton support the silhouettes' simple elegance. At the same time Emily Katz makes a statement regarding our rightful place within nature, which—according to the designer—must work with the natural cycle rather than against it. She uses environmentally friendly materials and has them manufactured locally in Portland.

Seit 2003 präsentiert die Designerin Emily Katz einzigartige Entwürfe, die sie aufwendig von Hand herstellen, färben und besticken lässt. Die Designerin setzt auf zeitloses und klassisches Design, das nicht aus der Mode kommen soll, und auf Kleidung, die man lange mit gutem Gewissen tragen kann. Das Label aus Portland, Oregon, präsentiert kleine, aber gewissenhafte Kollektionen mit drapierten Kleidern aus nachhaltigen und innovativen Materialien wie z.B. wasserfestem Vlies. Stoffe aus Soja-Jersey, Hanf, recyceltem Denim und organischer Baumwolle unterstützen die einfache Eleganz der Silhouetten. Dabei setzen sie zudem ein Statement bezüglich unseres Platzes in der Natur, der sich – der Designerin nach – ihrem Kreislauf einfügen und nicht gegen sie arbeiten soll. Emily Katz verwendet nicht nur umweltfreundliche Stoffe, sondern lässt alle Teile sozial gerecht vor Ort in Portland herstellen.

Emmeline 4 Re | Designer: Emmeline Child

Fall Winter 2007/08
www.emmeline4re.co.uk

Emmeline 4 Re is all about recycling fashion. Materials that would normally end up in the garbage are turned into unique and creative pieces. Preferred materials include wool, leather, and denim. However, just about everything that can be recycled is used, including buttons and decorations. Every item thus fashioned is totally individual. The label obtains its raw materials from second hand clothing collectors such as Kettering Textiles, who collect and distribute second hand clothing in the UK. But donations from friends, or factory remnants, are also most welcome. The materials are subject to thorough testing. Thus, Emmeline 4 Re guarantees not only an innovative design but also top quality recycled fashion. Its program includes women's collections as well as handmade shoes and accessories for dogs.

Bei Emmeline 4 Re dreht sich alles um das Recycling von Mode. Stoffe, die normalerweise auf Deponien landen, werden in kreative Einzelstücke verwandelt. Bevorzugte Materialien sind Wolle, Leder und Denim. Generell wird jedoch alles miteinbezogen, was zur Wiederverwertung geeignet ist, so auch Knöpfe und Verzierungen. Daraus entstehen innovative Unikate, denn kein recyceltes Bekleidungsstück gleicht dem anderen. Das Rohmaterial bezieht das Label von Altkleider-Sammelunternehmen, wie z.B. Kettering Textiles, die in Großbritannien gebrauchte und recycelte Kleidung sammeln und anbieten. Aber auch Spenden von Freunden, Kunden oder Fabrik-Restposten sind gerne gesehen. An die Stoffe werden trotzdem hohe Qualitätsansprüche gestellt. Sie werden nur nach einem gründlichen Check verarbeitet. So garantiert Emmeline 4 Re nicht nur ein innovatives Design, sondern auch eine hohe Qualität der Recyling-Mode. Im Angebot haben sie nicht nur Mode für Frauen, sondern sogar auch handgefertigte Schuhe und Accessoires für Hunde.

Enamore | Designer: Jenny Ambrose

Spring Summer 2008

www.enamore.co.uk

After fully realizing and comprehending the damage caused to the environment by the clothing industry, the fashion designer Jenny Ambrose had the idea of creating beautiful and playful apparel from organically grown or recycled materials. Her label Enamore presents enticing silk bodices, hemp bras, and soy briefs—all ecologically sound, yet sexy. Apart from this ethically correct line of underwear introduced in 2004, Jenny Ambrose also designs normal clothes. The pieces are not manufactured in cheap third world countries, but in Bath and London. The designer uses only organically produced and sustainable materials such as the best hemp, cotton, soy, or silk as a result. However, Enamore's undergarments are neither rough on the skin nor the eye. On the contrary: frilly briefs and lacy bras are soft to the touch and portray the wearer as a femme naturale and impart a bit of a sexy pin-up girl feeling. The collections match those of "Agent Provocateur" in all aspects including price.

Nachdem sich die Modedesignerin Jenny Ambrose der Schäden, die die Modeindustrie der Umwelt zufügt, bewusst wurde, war es ihre Vision, schöne, verspielte Kleidung aus organischen oder recycelten Materialien herzustellen. Mit Enamore präsentiert sie heute verführerische Seidenkorsagen, Hanf-BHs und Soja-Slips, die ökologisch korrekt und trotzdem sexy sind. Denn neben einer Kleiderkollektion entwirft die Designerin seit 2004 eine ethisch korrekte Unterwäschenlinie. Gefertigt werden die Teile nicht in kostengünstigen Ländern der Dritten Welt, sondern in Bath und London. Die Designerin verwendet rein organische und nachhaltige Materialien aus feinstem Hanf, Baumwolle, Soja oder Seide. Das macht die Dessous von Enamore aber weder kratzig noch bieder. Ganz im Gegenteil: Rüschen-Schlüpfer und Spitzen-BHs fühlen sich zart und weich an und verleihen seiner Trägerin die Ausstrahlung einer „Femme Naturale" oder die eines sexy Pin-Up Girls. Die Kollektionen stehen denen von „Agent Provocateur" auch hinsichtlich des Preises in nichts nach.

FIN | Designer: Per Åge Sivertsen

Fall Winter 2008/09

www.finoslo.com

The Scandinavian label FIN is synonymous with the term "Eco-Lux". The label was established in 2006 by Nikolai Perminow, Eivind Ødegård and Nicolai Herlofson. Today, Per Åge Sivertsen is the company's head designer. Top quality and contemporary design as well as qualitative and ecological awareness form the basis of the company's philosophy. FIN is on the cutting edge of luxurious eco textiles. The current collection uses certified eco cotton, the extremely valuable wool of the baby alpaca, bamboo, and hand picked wild silk. FIN thus combines top quality design with fair trade and environmentally friendly production processes, especially in terms of carbon emissions. FIN also ensures fair wages and good working conditions, and its workshops in India and Peru adhere to human rights. FIN fashion is fair and chic! The label's modern collection is presented at large fashion shows in Paris, Berlin, London, Stockholm, and Oslo.

Das skandinavische Label FIN prägt den Begriff „Eco-Lux". Gegründet wurde es von Nikolai Perminow, Eivind Ødegård and Nicolai Herlofson im Jahre 2006. Per Åge Sivertsen ist heute Chefdesigner von FIN. Hochwertiges und zeitgemäßes Modedesign sowie qualitatives und ökologisches Bewusstsein bilden die Basis der Unternehmensphilosophie. FIN ist Vorreiter in der Verwendung von luxuriösen Öko-Stoffen. Derzeit werden die Kollektionen aus zertifizierter Bio-Baumwolle, der äußerst wertvollen Wolle des Baby Alpakas, Bambus und handgepflückter Wildseide hergestellt. Dabei vereint FIN hochwertiges Design mit fairem Handel und umweltfreundlicher Produktion, insbesondere bezüglich der Reduzierung des CO_2-Ausstoßes. FIN sorgt zudem für gerechte Löhne, gute Arbeitsbedingungen und die Berücksichtigung der Menschenrechte in den Herstellerländern Indien und Peru. FIN Fashion ist fair und schick! Die modernen Kollektionen des Labels werden auf den großen Modemessen in Paris, Berlin, London, Stockholm und Oslo präsentiert.

IDOM | Designer: Modi Soondarotok
Fall Winter 2008/09
www.idomdesigns.com

Modi Soondarotok presented her first collection of her label IDOM in her IDOM boutique in Portland in 2006. The designer draws inspiration from her homeland of Thailand. She remains true to her native country in that she uses Thai weavers and tailors. The collections are produced locally using environmentally friendly textiles, which are colored with natural dyes. Direct contact with seamstresses guarantees fair wages and very good working conditions. The workers finish each piece by hand at home and create top quality, unique apparel. In her label IDOM, Modi combines creativity and quality with social responsibility. IDOM offers a wide variety of choice for the fashion conscious woman. Simple cuts and colorful textiles are so designed, that a multitude of variations and combinations are possible. Modi translates her feel for fashion into playful, yet modern and elegant design.

2006 präsentierte die Modedesignerin Modi Soondarotok die erste Kollektion ihres Labels IDOM in ihrer gleichnamigen IDOM-Boutique in Portland. Inspirieren lässt sich die Designerin in ihren Entwürfen von ihrer Heimat Thailand. Sie zeigt sich heimatverbunden und arbeitet direkt mit thailändischen Webern und Schneidern zusammen. Die Kollektionen werden vor Ort aus umweltfreundlichen Textilien hergestellt und mit natürlichen Färbemitteln koloriert. Der direkte Kontakt mit den Handwerkerinnen garantiert faire Löhne und sehr gute Arbeitsbedingungen. In Heimarbeit fertigen die Näherinnen jedes Stück von Hand und schaffen somit hochwertige Unikate. Modi verbindet in ihrem Label IDOM Kreativität und Qualität mit sozialer Verantwortung. IDOM bietet für modebewusste Frauen eine Vielzahl besondere Mode. Schlichte Schnitte und farbenfreudige Stoffe sind so angelegt, dass IDOM Kollektionsteile eine Vielzahl an Variationen und Kombinationen ermöglichen. Ihr Gespür für Mode setzt Modi verspielt und zugleich modern und elegant in ihrem Design um.

Ivana Basilotta

Spring Summer 2009 (page 39), Autumn Winter 2008/09 (page 40-41)
www.ivanabasilotta.co.uk

Ivana Basilotta, born in Italy but brought up in Germany, is one of London's up and coming fashion designers. In contrast to many of her innovative young colleagues, she uses natural and organic fabrics for her collections. Her Turkish and Indian suppliers boast the Oeco-Tex Standard 100 certificate by subjecting themselves to voluntary controls, which check on environmentally friendly production by the international "Oeco-Tex" institute. This way the designer can guarantee her pieces to be free from harmful pesticides and this good feeling translates to her designs, which exude a certain freshness and lightness of being. It is the expressed aim of this young fashion label to develop into one the largest modern, yet ethically correct and sustainable brands of the high end fashion market. From spring summer 2009 all the silk she use will be "peace silk." This silk is manufactured in a process where silkworms are not killed. The moths emerge from their cocoons to live out their full life cycle.

Die in Deutschland aufgewachsene Italienerin Ivana Basilotta zählt zu einer der aufstrebendsten Modedesigerinnen Londons. Im Gegensatz zu vielen ihrer innovativen, jungen Kollegen verwendet sie für ihre Kollektionen rein natürliche und organische Materialien. Ihre Zulieferer in Indien und der Türkei besitzen alle das Öko-Tex Standard 100 Zertifikat. Sie unterziehen ihre Herstellung freiwilligen Kontrollen auf eine umweltfreundliche Produktion durch das internationale Prüfinstitut „Öko-Tex". Somit kann die Designerin dafür garantieren, dass alle ihre Produkte frei von gesundheitsgefährdenden Schadstoffen sind. Dieses gute Gefühl strahlen ihre frischen Entwürfe durch eine gewisse Leichtigkeit aus. Ziel des jungen Modelabels ist es, sich in den nächsten Jahren zu einem der größten modernen und gleichzeitig ethisch korrekten und nachhaltigsten Modemarken im High-End Fashion Bereich zu etablieren. Mit der Frühjahr/Sommer Kollektion 2009 beginnt für Ivana Basilotta auch der Einsatz von „friedlicher Seide". Diese Seide wird in einem Herstellungsprozess gewonnen, bei dem keine Seidenraupen getötet werden.

Leila Hafzi

Spring Summer 2008 (page 43), Fall Winter 2008/09 (pages 44-45)
www.leila-hafzi.com

Leila Hafzi counts among Norway's most committed fashion designers. The autodidact did not attend a fashion college but learned by doing during her work with her production team Nepal Productions. Leila Hafzi extended her Nepal network over the last decade to such an extent that it includes the best local suppliers and manufacturers. In 1997 she presented her first eco collection and was the first to introduce the notion of ethically and ecologically sound actions to the Norwegian fashion industry. Leila Hafzi never took her eyes off her ultimate goal: to create an awareness for ethically and ecologically sound fashion within the global fashion market and to develop a 100% environmentally friendly production cycle. The designer not only works to her own exacting environmental standards but uses her environment and current problems as sources of inspiration. Her Fall/Winter collection 2008/09 "O3" translates the breaking up of the vitally important ozone layer into colors: sky blue and fuchsia colored apparel is supposed to represent the former vitality of the ozone layer, while designs in bilious green, violet, and black typify the damage being done to it. She uses only natural based and certified azo free dyes. What else could one expect?

Leila Hafzi zählt zu den engagiertesten Modedesignern Norwegens. Die Autodidaktin besuchte keine Modeschule, sondern erlernte ihr Fachwissen gemeinsam mit ihrem Produktions-Team Nepal Productions. Während der letzten zehn Jahre baute Leila Hafzi ihr Netzwerk in Nepal soweit aus, dass es heute die besten Materialhersteller und Produzenten vor Ort umfasst. 1997 präsentierte sie ihre erste Öko-Kollektion. Damit führte sie die Idee von ethisch und ökologisch gerechtem Handeln in der norwegischen Modebranche ein. Leila Hafzi ließ sich nie von ihrem Ziel abbringen, ein Bewusstsein für ethisch und ökologisch gerechte Mode in der weltweiten Modewelt schaffen und in Zukunft einen 100%-ig umweltfreundlichen Produktionskreislauf entwickeln zu wollen. Die Designerin handelt nicht nur umweltfreundlich, sondern lässt sich auch von der Umwelt und aktuellen Problematiken inspirieren. Ihre Herbst/Winter 2008/09 Kollektion „O3" übersetzt den Verfall der lebenswichtigen Ozonschicht in Farben: Himmelblaue und fuchsiafarbene Kleider sollen die einstige Vitalität der Ozonschicht sichtbar machen. Entwürfe in Giftgrün, Violett und Schwarz versinnbildlichen den aktuellen Schaden. Alle verwendeten Farben basieren auf natürlichen Farben und sind frei von krebserregenden AZO Farbstoffen, was sonst?!

Les Fées de Bengale | Designers: Sophie Dupuy, Camille Dupuy, Elodie le Derf

Fall Winter 2008/09
www.lesfeesdesbengale.fr

The elegant designs by the three young fashion designers, who call themselves Les Fées de Bengale—the fairies of Bengal—are beautiful to look at and on the inside, too, because the label stands for socially just production and environmentally friendly design. Each and every Les Fées de Bengale product is treated like an individual—be it hand woven or hand embroidered—from concept creation through to production. The desired effect is that each item of apparel is different—quite the opposite of mass production. The designers use natural and ecologically sound materials such as organic cotton or silk. Les Fées de Bengale not only create unique, fairy like fashion for women but support socially disadvantaged women in India. To this end, the designers work with two social organizations in Bombay and Tamil Nadu. Women in need receive training as seamstress so that they can earn their own money. Moreover, the women receive education and partake in a medical scheme.

Die eleganten Entwürfe der drei jungen Modedesignerinnen, die sich Les Fées de Bengale, zu deutsch „die Feen aus dem Bengal" nennen, zeichnen sich nicht nur durch ihre äußere, sondern auch durch ihre innere Schönheit aus. Denn die Marke steht für eine sozial gerechte Produktion und für umweltfreundliches Design. Von der Konzepterstellung bis hin zur Produktion wird ein jedes Produkt von Les Fées de Bengale individuell behandelt, handgewebt oder handbestickt. Dank der Handarbeit gleicht, im Gegensatz zur Massenproduktion, kein Kollektionsteil dem anderen. Für ihre einzigartigen Entwürfe verwenden die Designerinnen rein natürliche und ökologisch gerechte Materialien wie organische Baumwolle oder Seide. Les Fées de Bengale kreieren nicht nur einzigartige, feen-gleiche Mode für Frauen, sondern unterstützen auch sozial benachteiligte Frauen in Indien. Hierfür arbeiten die Designerinnen bei der Herstellung mit zwei sozialen Organisationen in Bombay und Tamil Nadu zusammen. Bedürftige Frauen erhalten eine Ausbildung als Näherin und können somit ihr eigenes Geld verdienen. Zudem erhalten die Frauen Fachwissen, Schulbildung und medizinische Versorgung.

Linea Designs | Designer: Jessica Beebe
Spring Summer 2006
www.lineadesigns.com

Purism and innovation are the mainstays of the American fashion label LINEA, established by fashion designer Jess Beebe in 2001. The plain fashion is cut romantically, yet cleverly. Her apparel is fashioned by local specialists and made from natural textiles. Sustainability of production paths and conserving traditional handicraft are also of great importance to her. Her collections are mainly made from organic wool, hemp, bamboo, and silk. LINEA takes a central role in Portland's up-and-coming young eco fashion scene. Jess Beebe counts among the most innovative young designers, who present their work twice a year at the famous Eco Fashion Week. She draws attention to environmentally friendly fashion and social responsibility in its production and throughout the USA. Jess Beebe's plain fashion is cut romantically, yet cleverly. Worth a special mention is the fact that she offers workshops and internships in her company to raise overall awareness of ecological fashion design.

Das im Jahr 2001 von der Modedesignerin Jess Beebe gegründete amerikanische Modelabel LINEA zielt auf Purismus und Innovation ab. Die schlichten Entwürfe besitzen einen romantischen Touch und sind raffiniert geschnitten. Die Kleidungsstücke werden aus natürlichen Fasern in lokalen Fachbetrieben produziert. Die Designerin legt auf Nachhaltigkeit in den Produktionswegen und die Erhaltung des traditionellen Handwerks besonderen Wert. In ihren Kollektionen verarbeitet sie vor allem organische Wolle, Hanf, Bambus und Seide. LINEA spielt in der aufkeimenden, jungen Ökomode-Szene Portlands eine wichtige Rolle. Jess Beebe zählt zu den innovativsten jungen Designern, die hier zweimal jährlich ihre Kollektionen auf der bekannten Eco-Fashionweek präsentieren und in den ganzen USA Aufmerksamkeit in Sachen sozial gerecht produzierter und umweltfreundlicher Mode erregen. Besonders bemerkenswert ist, dass sie in ihrem Betrieb Workshops und Praktika anbietet, durch die sie ihr ökologisches Bewusstsein in Sachen Modedesign weiterträgt.

Liza Rietz

Linen cross back jumper with balloon sleeve top
www.lizarietz.com

Liza Rietz came out with her first ecologically sound collection in 2001. The designer is part of the young and up-and-coming eco fashion scene in Portland, USA. She was one of the first to take part in independent fashion shows centered around the eco trend, and to support various ecological organizations. Her commitment paid off. These days her designs are exclusively available at the liza rietz showroom in Portland and for sale online at her website. Liza Rietz describes her pieces as feminine, wearable, and above all individual. Her hand-made unique clothing takes a stand against mass production and the ecological damage caused by it. All her products are based on natural materials such as cotton, linen, silk, and bamboo. The designer does not adhere to seasonal fashion trends, that is to say she does not present two collections a year. Instead she creates timeless sustainable fashion, which easily survives a season and remains modern and hip.

Liza Rietz präsentierte bereits 2001 ihre erste ökologisch gerechte Kollektion. Die Designerin ist Teil der jungen, aufstrebenden Ökomode-Szene in Portland, USA. Sie war eine der Ersten, die an unabhängigen Modeschauen rund um das Thema Öko teilnahm und sich in verschiedenen, umweltfreundlichen Organisationen engagierte. Das Engagement hat sich ausgezahlt. Heute sind ihre Entwürfe in dem eigenen Showroom in Portland oder auf ihrer Website im Online-Shop erhältlich. Ihre modernen Entwürfe beschreibt Liza Rietz selbst als feminin, tragbar und vor allem individuell. Mit ihren handgefertigten und einzigartigen Kleiden wendet sie sich gegen die Massenproduktion und deren bei der Produktion einhergehenden Umweltsünden. Alle Produkte haben als Basis natürliche Materialien wie Baumwolle, Leinen, Seide und Bambus. Die Designerin richtet sich nicht nach den Saisons, sprich sie zeigt nicht zwei Kollektionen pro Jahr, sondern kreiert zeitlose Mode, die über eine Saison hinaus modern, angesagt und trotzdem nachhaltig ist.

Lizzie Parker

Fall Winter 2008/09

www.lizzieparker.com

Lizzie Parker is an ecologically aware American fashion label for the modern woman. The designer demonstrates responsibility towards the environment by using only environmentally friendly materials for her elegant collections. The raw materials are mainly comprised of eco cotton and natural bamboo. The designer has her collections produced locally in factories in and around Seattle, thus avoiding long transit routes and supporting local firms at the same time. Lizzie Parker donates remnants and leftover materials to local charities. She is a member of the "1% for the Planet" community of small businesses, who voluntarily pay a 1% "earth tax" of their turnover to non-profit and non-governmental conservation groups. Lizzie Parker is among those who present designs at one of the USA's most famous eco-trade fairs, the Portland Fashion Week. The stylish and flattering items of clothing are marketed in America and Tokyo.

Lizzie Parker ist ein ökologisch bewusstes, modernes Label für Frauenbekleidung aus den USA. Die Designerin zeigt ökologische Verantwortung, indem sie rein umweltfreundliche Stoffe für ihre eleganten Kollektionen verwendet. Ihre Rohmaterialien sind aus Bio-Baumwolle und dem von Natur aus umweltfreundlichen Bambus. Die Designerin lässt ihre Kollektionen in lokalen Produktionsstätten im Umkreis von Seattle herstellen und vermeidet somit lange Transportwege und unterstützt zugleich ortsansässige Firmen. Materialüberschuss und Restposten spendet Lizzie Parker an örtliche Charity-Verbände. Sie ist Mitglied bei „1% for the Planet", einer Gemeinschaft kleiner Unternehmen, die freiwillig eine „Earth Steuer" bezahlen und 1% ihrer Umsätze an gemeinnützige und nichtstaatliche Umweltschutzorganisationen spenden. Lizzie Parker präsentiert ihr Design unter anderem auf einer der bekanntesten Öko-Messen der USA, der „Portland Fashion Week". Die schicken und schmeichelnden Kollektionsstücke sind nicht nur auf dem amerikanischen Kontinent vertrieben, sondern mittlerweile auch in Tokyo zu finden.

makeZenz | Founders: Julie Villumsen, Stine Sonne Bauer

Spring Summer 2009
www.makezenz.com

To stand in front of thousands of people dressed only in a bikini requires great courage. Julie Villumsen showed that she has what it takes, when she was Miss Earth representive for Denmark 2002. She used the contest to talk in front of a large audience about her love of fashion and the reasons why only organic cotton should be used. This was one of many steps the designer took to fight for a better world. Julie Villumsen presented her first makeZenz collection in Copenhagen in 2003. Even in those days the designer thought of conventional cotton as a second rate material and used only organically produced textiles. Julie Villumsen is very committed to makeZenz, a passion she shares with textile buyer Stine Bauer. The label produced its first collections in Denmark, but because of demand and lack of local workshops, it had to move its production to Poland. There, too, the apparel is manufactured by family-run businesses under socially just conditions. makeZenz sees itself not as a fashion label, but as a lifestyle brand—the reason why the two partners opened their first makeZenz concept store in 2006. This first "organic lifestyle boutique" markets its own collections as well as other internationally renowned eco designers, environmentally friendly jewelry, and natural cosmetics.

Nur in einem Bikini bekleidet vor tausenden Menschen zu stehen, erfordert großen Mut. Den bewies Julie Villumsen damals als sie bei der Wahl zur Miss Earth 2002 als Vertreterin Dänemarks auftrat. Sie nutze die Misswahl, um vor einer großen Menschenmenge über ihre Liebe zu Mode und über die Gründe, weswegen man rein organische Baumwolle verwenden sollte, sprechen zu können. Diese Aktion gehört zu einem von vielen Wegen, die die Designerin beschreitet, um für eine bessere Welt zu kämpfen. Die erste Kollektion von makeZenz präsentierte Julie Villumsen im August 2003 in Kopenhagen. Für die Designerin war herkömmliche Baumwolle schon damals Ware zweiter Wahl. Die umweltfreundlichen Aktivisten verwenden ausschließlich rein organische Materialien. Heute ist makeZenz für Julie Villumsen eine Leidenschaft, die sie mit der Textileinkäuferin Stine Bauer teilt. Die ersten Kollektionen produzierten makeZenz noch in Dänemark. Aufgrund steigender Nachfrage und kaum vorhandenen großen Produktionsstätten vor Ort, musste das Label seine Produktion nach Polen verlagern. Aber auch dort werden die Kollektionen sozial gerecht in einem Familienbetrieb gefertigt. Das Label sieht sich nicht als Mode-, sondern als Lifestyle-Marke. Deswegen eröffneten die beiden Partnerinnen 2006 den ersten makeZenz Concept-Store. Diese erste „Organic Lifestyle Boutique" bietet neben der eigenen Kollektion Mode international angesehene Öko-Designer, umweltfreundlichen Schmuck und natürliche Kosmetik an.

Mark Liu

Fall Winter 2008/09
www.markliu.co.uk

Mark Liu, brought up in Australia, is not only interested in fashion but also in science and philosophy. He researched new materials and nanotechnology within the fashion industry for his bachelor degree thesis. He read for a Master's degree in "Future Textile Technology" at the renowned "Central Saint Martins College of Art and Design" in London to broaden his knowledge in the field. Today Mark Liu is seen as the founder of "zero waste fashion," a production process that eliminates all remnants and waste material. Conventional tailoring wastes a minimum of 15% of the material used while his new cutting process results in zero waste. To achieve this, Mark Liu effectively had to reinvent pattern cutting techniques, and his new and innovative method enables the creation of imaginative new shapes without wasting fabric. The London based designer, who has worked for Alexander McQueen, for example, would like to raise awareness among his colleagues that sustainable, ecologically efficient design can also be modern.

Der in Australien aufgewachsene Mark Liu interessiert sich nicht nur für Mode, sondern auch für Wissenschaft und Philosophie. Für seine Diplomarbeit recherchierte er neue mögliche Materialien und Nanotechnologien in der Modeindustrie. Um seine Kenntnisse in diesem Bereich auszubauen, absolvierte er seinen Master im Bereich „Zukünftige Textiltechnologien" an dem renommierten Central Saint Martins College of Art and Design in London. Mark Liu gilt heute als Begründer der „Zero Waste Fashion", einer Modeproduktion ohne Ausschussware und Abfälle. Bei einem herkömmlichen Stoffzuschnitt werden 15% des verwendeten Materials zu Resten und damit zu Abfallprodukten. Mark Liu´s Schnitte verursachen beim Zuschnitt keine Stoffreste. Dafür musste er alle Regeln der Schnitttechnik brechen und neu erfinden. Mit dieser innovativen Methode schafft er fantasievolle, neue Formen, ohne Stoff verschwenden zu müssen. Der heute in London lebende Designer, der unter anderem für Alexander McQueen tätig war, will heute bei seinen Kollegen ein Bewusstsein für die Möglichkeiten von nachhaltigem, ökologisch effizientem Design, das auf Modernität nicht verzichten muss, schaffen.

MILCH | Designer: Cloed Priscilla Baumgartner

Fall Winter 2007/08

www.milch.mur.at

Fashion designer Cloed Priscilla Baumgartner is the name behind the MILCH label. She does not intend to add to the already considerable "clothing mountain" by creating yet another new collection. That is why MILCH applies the "upcycling" principle and reuses remnants and other items in new ways. Classic male suits are thus converted to women's trousers or blouses—a clever and purposeful confusion between the sexes. Production processes for MILCH are short and simple: men's trousers and shirts from clothes collections by the used clothing collection Vienna serve as raw materials. Manufacturing itself takes place in Vienna with seamstresses working from home. Every piece is therefore a unique item. The winter collection KNITTERHEMDKLEIDER 2007/08 shows knitted clothing, whose origins, namely remnants or thrown away items, can only be guessed at even on second glance. The designer cut all kinds of old men's shirts in strips and knitted them together to form thick, warm pieces suitable for the time of year.

Hinter dem Label MILCH steht die Modedesignerin Cloed Priscilla Baumgartner. Sie will den bereits bestehenden „Wäscheberg" mit der Kreation neuer Kollektionen nicht noch vergrößern. Deswegen wird seit 1998 bei MILCH ausgemusterte Ware durch das Prinzip des „Upcycling" in einem anderen Kontext wiederverwendet. Einen klassischen Männeranzug verwandelt die Designerin z.B. zu Hosen- und Hemdkleidern für Damen – ein beabsichtigt verwirrendes Spiel zwischen den Geschlechtern. Die Produktionswege sind bei MILCH kurz und einfach: als Rohmaterial dienen Herrenhosen und Herrenhemden aus dem Altkleidercontainer. Dieses wird von der Volkshilfe Wien gesammelt und dem Label zur Verfügung gestellt. Gefertigt werden die MILCH-Produkte dann direkt in Wien in Heimarbeit. So wird ein jedes Kollektionsteil zum individuellen Unikat. Die Winterkollektion KNITTERHEMDKLEIDER 2007/08 zeigt Strickwaren, denen man erst auf den zweiten Blick ihre Herkunft – nämlich ausgemusterte, weggeworfene Abfallhemden – ansieht. Alle möglichen Herrenhemden hat die Designerin in Streifen geschnitten und passend zur Jahreszeit zu dicken, warmen Maschen verstrickt.

naturevsfuture® | Designer: Nina Valenti

Fall Winter 2008/09

www.naturevsfuture.com

Nina Valenti founded the American fashion label "naturevsfuture®" in 2002. In the designer's eyes there is an eternal struggle between nature and the future, a fact she expresses in her label's name and addresses in her collections, where she attempts to find the right balance between nature and technology. Season after season she increases the proportion of organic, sustainable, renewable, and biodegradable materials: eco wool and cotton, hemp, soy, bamboo, seacell®, lyocell (cellulose), and Ingeo™, as well as recycled and synthetic materials such as Polartec®. Her pieces are manufactured in New York and Peru sold throughout the USA, although markets in Canada, Italy, Japan, and Singapore have also shown interest in "naturevsfuture®". The innovative, sculptural fashion made from natural and renewable materials is much sought after, especially by socialites and celebrities, as well as a number of publications. In answer to overwhelming demand, Valenti works on ecologically correct wedding and evening attire and plans a men's line for Fall 2009.

Das amerikanische Modelabel „naturevsfuture®" wurde 2002 von Nina Valenti gegründet. Für die Designerin besteht ein beständiger Kampf zwischen Natur und Zukunft. Mit ihrem Labelnamen drückt sie dies aus und in ihren Kollektionen versucht sie die richtige Balance zwischen organischen und technischen Kräften zu finden. Jede Saison setzt sie mehr organische, nachhaltige, erneuerbare und biologisch abbaubare Materialien ein: organische Wolle und Baumwolle, Hanf, Soja, Bambus, Seacell®, Lyocell, einer Faser auf Zellstoffbasis, und Ingeo™, aber auch recycelte und technische Materialien wie z.B. Polartec®, einem Fleecematerial. Die Teile werden in New York und Peru angefertigt, hauptsächlich in den USA vertrieben, aber auch schon in Kanada, Italien, Japan und Singapur stößt „naturevsfuture®" auf Interesse. Die innovative, skulpturale Mode aus natürlichen und nachhaltigen Stoffen von „naturevsfuture®" stößt in diversen Publikationen auf positive Resonanz und ist auch bei VIP's sehr beliebt. Derzeit arbeitet Nina Valenti auf Wunsch ihrer Kunden an ökologisch gerechten Hochzeits- und Abendkleidern und plant für Herbst 2009 ihre erste Herrenkollektion.

Noir | Founder, Designer: Peter Ingwersen

Fall Winter 2008/09 (pages 66-69), Fall Winter 2007/08 (page 69 large)
www.noir-illuminati2.com

Danish designer Peter Ingwersen demonstrates that fashion produced through environmentally friendly practices and socially acceptable conditions is sexy, provoking, and luxurious. His main aim in founding the label Noir in 2005 was sustainability. He also created his own eco cotton production in Uganda. From 2008, the designer will be making his material collection, Illuminate2, available to selected clients in the textile industry. The Illuminate2 brand positions, markets, and sells bio-cotton from Uganda with the aim of providing the world's best cotton without cutting corners. The cotton is traded fairly and workers' minimum wages are guaranteed. Farmers in Africa receive a little more money than usual and are therefore able to spend a little more, too. This way the living standards of a whole society are steadily improved. A share of the profits of both firms flows back to the Noir-foundation, which provides social and medical support for local workers. Education and credit schemes enable autonomous development of the local infrastructure. The designer's current plans include the introduction of a new, sexy label in the medium price range called Black Noir. Same values, same look. But the really expensive stuff is left out: no silk, no leather—everybody can afford it! Peter Ingwersen says, "I believe that fashion can be beautiful, both from the outside and the inside!"

Der dänische Designer Peter Ingwersen hat bewiesen, dass Mode, die umwelt- und sozialverträglich entstanden ist, sexy, provokant und luxuriös aussehen kann. Vor allem vor dem Hintergrund der Nachhaltigkeit gründete er 2005 das Label Noir und eine eigene Produktion für ökologische Baumwolle in Uganda. Seit 2008 bietet der Designer seine Stoffkollektion „Illuminati2" auch ausgesuchten Kunden aus der Textilbranche an. Die Marke positioniert, vermarktet und verkauft Bio-Baumwolle aus Uganda, mit dem Ziel, ohne Kompromisse die besten Baumwollstoffe der Welt anbieten zu können. Die Baumwolle wird fair gehandelt, Mindestlöhne sind garantiert. Die Farmer in Afrika bekommen etwas mehr Geld und können etwas mehr Geld ausgeben. Auf diese Art hebt sich langsam der Lebensstandard einer ganzen Gesellschaft. Gewinnanteile aus beiden Firmen fließen in die Noir-Foundation, die wiederum die lokalen Mitarbeiter sozial und medizinisch absichert. Ausbildungsmöglichkeiten und Kleinkredite ermöglichen die Entwicklung der lokalen Infrastruktur in Eigenregie. Jetzt will der Designer Black Noir, ein sehr sexy Label im mittleren Preissegment, einführen. Die gleichen Werte, der gleiche Look. Nur die ganz teuren Details fehlen. Keine Seide, kein Leder. Dafür kann es sich jeder leisten. Peter Ingwersen: „Ich glaube daran, dass Mode schön sein kann – von außen und auch von innen!"

People Tree | Founder: Safia Minney

Spring Summer 2008
www.peopletree.co.uk

The People Tree label presented its first eco line in Japan as early as 1997—a case in point that fashion can be exciting and discerning without harming either humans or the planet. The label offers a wide choice of products, including lines for ladies, men, kids and babies, accessories, and even household articles. All products comply to the most stringent Fair-Trade and environmental standards. People Tree started cooperating with internationally renowned designers in 2007—a clever move, which has seen them become a reputable label on the international stage. The current collection includes exclusive designs by London's new star designers Richard Nicoll and Bora Aksu, and New York's Thakoon Panichgul. The pieces are sown by hand in India, using local cotton and colored with natural dyes. Fair-Trade in People Tree speak means paying far more than what elsewhere is considered fair wages. People Tree supports organic cotton farming—50% of their collections are made from eco cotton. Together with 50 Fair-Trade producers in 15 developing countries, the label gives a helping hand to some 2000 farmers and trades people. People Tree provides technical equipment, supports education drives and traditional artisan skills such as weaving, knitting, and embroidery.

Das Label People Tree präsentierte seine erste Öko-Linie bereits 1997 in Japan und ist ein Beweis dafür, dass Mode aufregend und anspruchsvoll sein kann, ohne den Menschen und unseren Planeten vernachlässigen zu müssen. Die Marke bietet ein breitgefächertes Angebot, von Damen-, Herren-, Kinder- und Babybekleidung über Accessoires bis hin zu Haushaltswaren. Alle Produkte entsprechen höchsten Fair-Trade- und Umweltstandards. Seit 2007 kooperiert People Tree mit international renommierten Designern und schafft es so zum international angesehenen Modelabel. Die aktuelle Kollektion zeigt exklusive Entwürfe von Londons neuen Lieblingsdesignern Richard Nicoll und Bora Aksu und des New Yorker Designers Thakoon Panichgul. Die Teile werden in Indien von Hand aus lokaler Baumwolle hergestellt und ausschließlich mit natürlichen Färbemitteln behandelt. Fair-Trade bedeutet für People Tree weit mehr als faire Löhne zu bezahlen. People Tree fördert den Anbau von organischer Baumwolle, aus der immerhin 50% der Kollektionen bestehen. Das Label unterstützt derzeit 2000 Farmer und Handwerker mit Hilfe von 50 Fair-Trade Produzenten in 15 Entwicklungsländern. People Tree stellt vor Ort technische Ausrüstung, fördert Bildungsmaßnahmen und traditionelle, handwerkliche Fähigkeiten wie Weben, Stricken und Sticken.

Rianne De Witte

Fall Winter 2008/09, Fall Winter 2003/04 (page 75 small pictures)
www.riannedewitte.nl

The Dutch fashion designer Rianne de Witte uses her label to contribute actively to sustainability in the fashion industry. She works together with Made-by, an organization that connects suppliers and producers who follow the principles of sustainability. All of Rianne de Witte's work is Fair-Trade certified and produced in the Netherlands, Poland, Portugal, Romania or Peru. The label is currently working towards the Made-by tracking system, which entails detailed information on where and how every single piece was manufactured. Rianne de Witte is aware that eco is not always the best tool for the job and that high quality and environmentally friendly man-made fibers are also available. This is reflected in her collections, which include not only linen, hemp, wool, and eco cotton but also environmentally responsibly produced synthetic accessories. Her current collection is the first to include high tech textiles made from 100% organic fiber, corn (PLA) from Ingeo. In 2007 Rianne de Witte opened her store in Breda, the Netherlands, where you can buy her label and several other brands.

Die niederländische Modedesignerin Rianne de Witte möchte mit ihrem Label aktiv zum Thema Nachhaltigkeit in der Modebranche beitragen. Sie arbeitet zusammen mit der Organisation Made-by, die Lieferanten und Produzenten an Modefirmen vermittelt, die für diese auf nachhaltige Weise produzieren. Alle Kleidungsstücke von Rianne de Witte sind Fair Trade zertifiziert und werden in den Niederlanden, Polen, Portugal, Rumänien oder Peru produziert. Derzeit strebt das Unternehmen das „Tracking"-System von Made-by an. Für zukünftige Kollektionen bedeutet dies, dass zu jedem einzelnen Stück detailliert nachvollzogen werden kann, wie und wo es produziert wurde. Rianne de Witte ist sich der Tatsache bewusst, dass Bio nicht immer 100% das Beste ist, sondern es auch hochwertige und umweltgerecht hergestellte Chemiefasern gibt. Ihre Kollektionen sind deswegen nicht nur aus Leinen, Hanf, Wolle und Bio-Baumwolle gearbeitet, sondern werden mit umweltfreundlich hergestellten, synthetischen Accessoires ergänzt. In ihrer aktuellen Kollektion verwendet die Designerin erstmals High-Tech-Gewebe, das aus 100% organischen Fasern, Mais (PLA) von Ingeo besteht. 2007 eröffnete Rianne de Witte ihren ersten eigenen Laden in Breda, den Niederlanden, in dem neben ihrem eigenen auch weitere Marken erhältlich sind.

Satoshi Date

Spring Summer 2008
www.satoshidate.com

Born in Japan, Satoshi Date studied fashion design at the famous "Central Saint Martins College of Art and Design" in London. He incorporates a multitude of aspects from the arts like painting, music, photography, and video art into his exciting fashion collections. These special collections also combine the hearing, seeing, and touching senses in a new and unique way by means of the materials used. Satoshi Date's fashion is admired for its special shapes and textures. His creations are partly made from home-made felt, eco wool, or hand painted textiles. He is against mass produced fashion and advocates hand made apparel—it is, after all, individual and precious. His work has been exhibited in London and Tokyo, and he presented his spring/summer collection during the London Fashion Week. He exhibits his ecologically correct design on special eco-flairs such as the "Ethical Fashion Show" in Paris, 2008.

Der gebürtige Japaner Satoshi Date studierte Modedesign an dem berühmten „Central Saint Martins College of Art and Design" in London. In seine spannenden Modekollektionen bezieht er eine Vielfalt von Aspekten aus Kunst, Malerei, Musik, Fotografie und Videokunst mit ein. In diesen speziellen Kollektionen vereint der Designer die Sinne Hören, Sehen und Fühlen miteinander und belebt sie auf neue und einzigartige Weise durch die dafür verwendeten Stoffe. Satoshi Dates Mode wird für ihre besonderen Formen und Texturen bewundert. Seine Kreationen sind zum Teil aus selbst hergestelltem Filz, ökologischer Wolle oder handbemaltem Gewebe gefertigt. Er wendet sich gegen die Massenproduktion von Mode hin zu handgemachten Textilien, denn diese sind individuell und kostbar. Die Arbeiten von Satoshi Date wurden bereits in London und Tokyo ausgestellt. Seine Frühjahr/Sommer-Kollektion präsentierte der Designer auf der London Fashion Week. Außerdem zeigt er sein außergewöhnlich ökologisch bewusstes Design auf modernen Öko-Messen wie zuletzt 2008 auf der „Ethical Fashion Show" in Paris.

Sublet | Inessah Selditz, Tara Eisenberg

Spring Summer 2008

ww.subletclothing.com

Sublet Clothing as a company is a means for positive social change. This American label displays both social and ecological awareness in production and management. The designer duo Inessah and Tara has long been active in conservation and sees its work in the fashion industry as a means to make a positive contribution to a possible fundamental change in their industry. Using ethical principles, the company manages sustainable production, superior design, a comfortable fit, and eclectic style—all created and produced locally in New York. Sublet Clothing offers wearable, modern clothing for ecologically aware customers. Their pieces are mainly made from organic cotton and bamboo. Sublet Clothing's mission is to be the go-to source for stylish and truly wearable clothing for the modern eco-minded consumer.

Sublet Clothing sieht seine Mode als Mittel für einen positiven, sozialen Wandel. Das amerikanische Label zeigt ein soziales und ökologisches Bewusstsein in der Herstellung und Leitung seines Unternehmens. Das Designer-Duo Inessah und Tara setzt sich schon lange aktiv für den Umweltschutz ein und sieht nun in seiner Arbeit mit Mode die Möglichkeit, etwas Gutes zu einem gesellschaftlichen Wandel in der Modebranche beitragen zu können. Eine nachhaltige Produktion, anspruchsvolles Design, bequeme Passformen und ein eklektischer Stil werden mit ethisch korrekten Mitteln konzipiert und vor Ort in New York City hergestellt. Sublet Clothing bietet tragbare, moderne Bekleidung für den ökologisch bewussten Käufer. Ihre Kollektionsteile werden hauptsächlich aus organischer Baumwolle und Bambus gefertigt. Transparenz ist den Designerinnen wichtig, so kann die Käuferin im Onlineshop bei jedem Kleidungsstück nachvollziehen, in welchem Verhältnis die unterschiedlichen Materialien eingesetzt werden.

VAN MARKOVIEC | Designers: Kasia Markowska, Zuzia Andziak

Spring Summer 2008

www.markoviec.com

The Dutch label VAN MARKOVIEC is for women who lead a sustainable lifestyle and want to be fashionably dressed. Nature with its breadth and complexity, its manifold shapes, colors, and structures provides sheer endless inspiration to the designers Kasia Markowska and Zuzia Andziak. They decided to start a fashion label that respects human rights and the environment and carried on to produce their collections in an ethically sound and environmentally friendly manner. The label therefore produces unique fashion of high quality that stands for social and ecological responsibility. Its collections make exclusive use of materials such as eco cotton, natural silk, and hemp as well as natural dyes. For the most part, the collections are made by European manufacturers, who follow the maxim of sustainability. VAN MARKOVIEC continues to use new and better quality materials season after season in order to meet their ecological standards.

Das niederländische Label VAN MARKOVIEC bietet Mode für Frauen, die einen nachhaltigen Lebensstil führen und zudem modisch gekleidet sein möchten. Die Natur mit ihrer Weite und Komplexität und der Vielfalt an Formen, Farben und Strukturen, ist für die Designerinnen Kasia Markowska und Zuzia Andziak eine nie versiegende Quelle inspirierender Impulse. Die Designerinnen entschieden sich, ein Modelabel zu gründen, das die Menschenrechte und die Umwelt achtet. So produzieren sie ihre Kollektionen ethisch gerecht und umweltbewusst. Auf diese Weise bringt das Label ein einzigartiges Modedesign in guter Qualität auf den Markt, das zugleich für soziales und ökologisches Verantwortungsbewusstsein steht. Für ihre Kollektionen verwenden sie Stoffe, die aus Öko-Baumwolle, Naturseide und Hanf bestehen und mit pflanzlichen Farben eingefärbt werden. Der größte Teil kommt von europäischen Herstellern, die eine nachhaltige Produktion verfolgen. Von Saison zu Saison setzt VAN MARKOVIEC neuere und hochwertigere Textilien ein, um den ökologischen Maßstäben gerecht zu werden.

Viridis Luxe | Hala Bahmet

Spring Summer 2008 (page 85), Fall Winter 2007/08 (page 86-87)
www.viridisluxe.com

VIRIDIS LUXE is a luxury eco label founded by Hala Bahmet in the USA in 2006. Her designs reflect her interest in unusual colors and constructions, as well as inspirations gathered from all over the world. Environmentally friendly materials and sustainability play a very important part in her work. VIRIDIS LUXE gives the eco trend a touch of glamour. The designer uses mainly hemp, the "greenest" of all textile fibers, and mixtures of bamboo and organic cotton, bamboo and cashmere, or hemp and cashmere. Production sites are controlled by Hala Bahmet personally, who checks both working conditions and quality of production. With her line she wants to contribute to the concept of sustainability and increase the environmental awareness of her customers. "Viridis" is the Latin for "green". The name thus emblematizes her label's aim of combining attractive and innovative design with environmentally friendly materials and ethical and sustainable production processes. Plans for a line of men's and kids' fashions are in the pipeline.

VIRIDIS LUXE ist ein Öko-Luxus-Label, das 2006 von Hala Bahmet in den USA gegründet wurde. Ihr Design spiegelt ihr Interesse an ungewöhnlichen Farben, Konstruktionen und Inspiration aus aller Welt wider. Dabei sind umweltfreundliche Materialien und Nachhaltigkeit stets von großer Bedeutung. VIRIDIS LUXE verleiht Öko-Mode einen glamourösen Charakter. Für ihre Kollektionen verwendet die Designerin vor allem Hanf, die „grünste" aller Textilfasern, Mischungen aus Bambus und Bio-Baumwolle, Bambus und Kaschmir oder Hanf und Kaschmir. Die Produktionsstätten werden hinsichtlich Qualität und Arbeitsbedingungen von Hala Bahmet regelmäßig persönlich kontrolliert. Mit ihrer Linie möchte sie nicht nur aktiv etwas zum Thema „Nachhaltigkeit" beitragen, sondern auch das Umweltbewusstein ihrer Kundinnen beeinflussen. „Viridis" ist lateinisch und bedeutet „Grün". So versinnbildlicht der Name des Labels das Ziel schickes und innovatives Design mit umweltfreundlichem Material und ethischen und nachhaltigen Produktionstechniken zu vereinen. Für die Zukunft plant das Label den Aufbau einer Männerlinie und Mode für Kinder.

adidas

Fall Winter 2008/09
www.adidas.com

adidas brought its "Green Collection" to the market in spring 2008. The company has joined the list of those global corporations picking up on the sustainability trend. This special product line is adidas' contribution to reducing its environmental impact by using the world's natural resources more efficiently. adidas Green thus reacts to increasing awareness of the environment and the importance of sustainable manufacturing methods. The collection consists of environmentally friendly recycled materials such as hemp and bamboo, and works with natural dyes. Recycled cotton clothing and hoodies of recycled polyester give the words „green" and „eco" a sporty and fashionable touch. It is often rumored that large textile companies supposedly go eco for PR reasons only because visible political correctness in a single line will extend across the whole product range. However, what it is far more important is that with its global presence and worldwide target audience, adidas contributes to instilling an awareness of sustainable products.

Seit Frühjahr 2008 präsentiert adidas seine „Grün Kollektion". Somit zählt das Unternehmen zu einem der Weltkonzerne, die derzeit beginnen, ein Gespür für nachhaltige Produkte zu entwickeln. Mit dieser speziellen Linie will adidas Originals einen kleinen Beitrag dafür leisten, die Umweltbelastung durch den effizienten Einsatz der natürlichen Ressourcen der Erde zu reduzieren. adidas Grün reagiert damit auf das steigende Umweltbewusstsein und das Wissen um die Bedeutung nachhaltiger Herstellungsverfahren. Die Kollektion besteht aus umweltfreundlichen und recycelten Materialien wie Hanf und Bambus, die Farben sind natürlichen Ursprungs. Kleider aus wiederverwerteten Baumwollresten und Kapuzen-Tops aus recyceltem Polyester verleihen den Worten „Grün" und „Öko" einen sportiven und modischen Touch. Oft heißt es, dass kleine Öko-Linien bei großen Modeunternehmen nur aus Imagegründen präsentiert werden, denn politisch korrektes Verhalten im kleinen Warenangebot kann auf das Große seinen Glanz werfen. Viel wichtiger aber ist, dass adidas aufgrund seiner globalen Präsenz mit seiner „Grün Kollektion" dazu beiträgt, bei seiner Zielgruppe weltweit ein Bewusstsein für nachhaltige Produkte zu schaffen.

armedangels | Founders: Anton Jurina, Martin Höfeler, Designer: Janosch Wengenroth
Spring Summer 2008
www.armedangels.de

armedangels—eco, social, and fair! Eco materials and Fair-Trade production are the hallmarks of this German fashion label. The designers from Cologne take a firm stand against child labor, exploitation, and pollution. This starts with cotton production in India and is applied right through to the manufacturing in Portugal. From September onwards armedangels supports three different relief projects. With the purchase of each shirt the buyer can decide which one his money should go to: to the education project ‚Pratham' in India, to the Bionade "Trinkwasserwald" (drinking water wood) near Berlin or to an Indian drinking water project, which the label supports in collaboration with Viva con Agua. armedangels is not just about fashion trends; the company also wants to lead the way when it comes to sustainability by fighting for better manufacturing conditions. The designers apply these principles rigorously, starting with such basics as avoiding wastage and using eco electricity. The company website serves as an additional platform with blog and its own community to further the "social fashion revolution". armedangels is proof that fair fashion can be stylish, too!

armedangels – bio, sozial und fair! Bio in den Materialien und Fair-Trade zertifiziert in der Produktion sind die Kennzeichen des deutschen Modelabels. Das Label aus Köln richtet sich konsequent gegen Kinderarbeit, Ausbeutung und Umweltverschmutzung. Das fängt beim Baumwollanbau in Indien an und setzt sich im gesamten Herstellungsprozess bis in die Näherei in Portugal fort. Ab September unterstützen armedangels drei unterschiedliche Hilfsprojekte. Mit dem Kauf eines Shirts kann der Kunde gleichzeitig selbst entscheiden, wohin sein Geld fließen soll: entweder in das Bildungsprojekt „Pratham" in Indien, an den Bionade-Trinkwasserwald bei Berlin oder in ein indisches Trinkwasserprojekt, das das Label zusammen mit Viva con Agua unterstützt. armedangels geht es nicht nur um modische Trends, sondern auch darum, ein Vorbild in Sachen Nachhaltigkeit zu sein, indem sie für bessere Produktionsbedingungen kämpfen und ihre Werte auch im Kleinen umsetzen. Dieses Bewusstsein beginnt bei der Müllvermeidung und hört beim Ökostrom noch lange nicht auf. Die Website dient zusätzlich als Plattform mit Blog und eigener Community um die „social fashion revolution" voranzutreiben. armedangels beweist, dass faire Mode auch stylisch sein kann!

this is an armedangels original made of 100 percent original fairtrade percent in with 100 cotto cent love 100 perc so hand care

BLAKE HAMSTER

Blake Hamster | Founders: FELD M, Designliga

All year/non seasonal collection, Release 0001, designer: Jeroen Jongeleen aka Influenza (page 95), Hamansutra (page 96, 97 above), Diana Keller & Damir Doma (page 97 below)

ww.blakehamster.com

Blake Hamster was created by the Munich based agencies FELD M and Designliga and markets original designs combined with a social and ecological sense of responsibility. The brand experiments with a variety of products, production processes and distribution strategies, while adhering to ethical and aesthetic standards at all times. Currently, Blake Hamster is presenting a limited T-shirt collection. The label's raw materials are comprised mainly of bio cotton. The ladies' tops are refined with Seacell, an innovative fiber that emits pleasant, active substances. It releases moisture to the skin and acts as skin care, toner, and as anti-inflammatory agent. The shirts are manufactured by a renowned family-run business in Italy. The socially acceptable pieces produced in an environmentally friendly manner may cost a little more, but the wearer pays for a clear conscience and a truly individual shirt. To guarantee a strong design, Blake Hamster involves a number of artists in the production of its sustainable products. For example, Blake Hamster launched a competition for its 2006 collection. The six best entries—by such renowned international figures as the Viennese artist Stephan Doehsinger or the Berlin-based musician Catriona Shaw, aka Miss LeBomb—were used for the line of that year.

Blake Hamster wurde von den Münchener Agenturen FELD M und Designliga ins Leben gerufen und präsentiert heute originelle Designs mit sozialem und ökologischem Verantwortungsbewusstsein. Die Marke will mit verschiedenen Produkten, Produktionsprozessen und Distributionsstrategien experimentieren. Dabei sollen stets ethische und ästhetische Grundregeln eingehalten werden. Aktuell präsentiert Blake Hamster eine limitierte T-Shirt Kollektion. Als Rohmaterialien verwendet das Label weitestgehend Baumwolle aus ökologischem Anbau. Die Damen Shirts wurden mit Seacell, einer innovativen Faser, die während des Tragens wohltuende aktive Substanzen an die Haut abgibt und damit Feuchtigkeit spendend, pflegend, straffend und entzündungshemmend wirkt, veredelt. Genäht werden die Shirts von einem renommierten Familienbetrieb in Italien. Die sozial gerecht produzierten und ökologisch gerechten Teile kosten zwar etwas mehr, aber der Träger wird mit einem guten Gewissen und einem individuell designten Shirt entlohnt. Um den Designaspekt hoch zu halten, bindet Blake Hamster viele verschiedene Kreative in den Entstehungsprozess seiner nachhaltigen Produkte mit ein. Für die Designs dieser Kollektion rief Blake Hamster 2006 einen Wettbewerb aus, dessen beste sechs Print-Ideen realisiert wurden. Zu den Gewinnern des Wettbewerbs zählen unter anderen der Wiener Künstler Stephan Doehsinger oder die Berliner Musikerin Catriona Shaw aka Miss LeBomb.

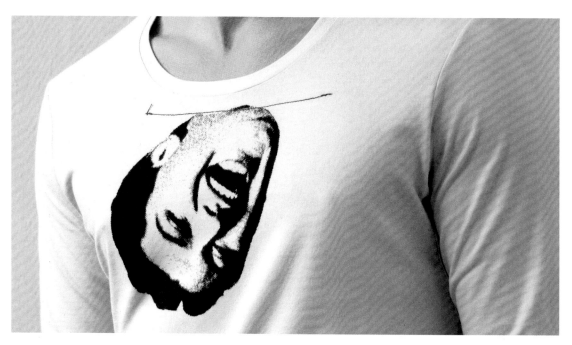

EDUN | Founders: Bono, Ali Hewson

Spring Summer 2008 (page 99), Fall Winter 2008/09 (pages 100-101)
www.edunonline.com

EDUN is a socially aware clothing company established in spring 2005 by the Irish singer and U2 front man Bono and his wife Ali Hewson. The company encourages economic growth in developing countries by awarding production contracts to factories in Asia, South America, and India. Regular tests by non-profit monitoring and training organizations such as Verité as well as visits to the factory by in-house EDUN staff guarantee socio-politically sound working conditions. Currently EDUN is manufacturing in India, Peru, Tunisia, Kenya, Uganda, Madagascar, and Mauritius. The use of ecologically produced cotton is axiomatic. For example, the Fall/Winter collection 2007 contained 31% organically produced materials. This figure increased to 50% for the Spring/Summer collection 2008. EDUN, read it backwards to get "nude", is not sold in ecological shops but is distributed in top department stores, such as New York Barney's or Harvey Nichols, for example. In principle, EDUN seeks to lead the way for those great designers who have not yet embraced the issue of ecology.

EDUN ist ein sozial engagiertes Modeunternehmen, das im Frühjahr 2005 von dem irischen Sänger Bono von U2 und seiner Frau Ali Hewson gegründet wurde. Die Firma fördert das Wirtschaftswachstum in Entwicklungsländern, indem sie Fabriken in Asien, Südamerika und Indien zur Produktion ihrer Kollektionen beauftragt. Prüfungen durch gemeinnützige Überwachungs- und Ausbildungsorganisationen wie Verité, sowie Werksbesuche durch interne EDUN Mitarbeiter finden regelmäßig statt und garantieren sozialpolitisch korrekte Arbeitsbedingungen. Derzeit produziert EDUN in Indien, Peru, Tunesien, Kenia, Uganda, Madagaskar und Mauritius. Bei der Herstellung wird großen Wert auf die Verarbeitung von Bio-Baumwolle gelegt. Somit besteht die Herbst/Winter-Kollektion 2007 zu 31%, die Frühjahr/Sommer Kollektion 2008 zu 50% aus organisch hergestellten Materialien. EDUN, das rückwärts gesprochen für „nude", also „nackt" steht, wird nicht in Öko-Läden, sondern unter anderem in dem New Yorker Nobelkaufhaus Barneys und bei Harvey Nichols verkauft. Grundsätzlich will EDUN Vorbild für die großen Designhäuser sein, die sich dem Thema Ökologie bislang so gut wie überhaupt nicht gewidmet haben.

Environmental Justice Foundation | Founders: Steve Trent, Juliette Williams

Suzanne Diaz wears Katharine Hamnett for EJF (page 103), Lisa Cant wears Betty Jackson design for EJF (page 104),
Irina Lazareanu wears Luella design for EJF (page 105)
www.ejfoundation.org

The non-profit, politically independent "Environmental Justice Foundation" (EJF) has launched its latest campaign, Pick Your Cotton Carefully! with the aim of raising awareness of crimes against the environment and human rights abuses in the cotton production industry. This socially conscientious and ecologically active organization is especially committed to bringing child labor to an end and stopping the use of dangerous pesticides during cotton production. Renowned designers such as Luella Bartley, Christian Lacroix, Betty Jackson, and Katharine Hamnett support the current project and submitted exclusive prints for a T-shirt collection made from organic and fairly traded cotton. More than 20 top models were prepared to support the good cause and had their pictures taken wearing the innovative T-shirts. The prints illustrated the issue of child labor, designed to the theme of "childhood, lost innocence and hope". The T-shirts drive home the message that over a million children worldwide have to work in cotton production against their will. All proceeds from the T-shirt collection, which is available from the organization's website, go to supporting EJF's charity work.

Die gemeinnützige, politisch unabhängige „Environmental Justice Foundation" (EJF) initiiert derzeit die Kampagne „Pick Your Cotton carefully!" Ziel ist es, weltweit auf Umweltsünden und den Missbrauch von Menschenrechten bei der Baumwollproduktion aufmerksam zu machen. Die sozial und umweltfreundlich engagierte Organisation setzt sich hierbei vor allem für das Aus von Kinderarbeit und den Gebrauch gefährlicher Pestizide bei der Herstellung von Baumwolle ein. Renommierte Designer wie Luella Bartley, Christian Lacroix, Betty Jackson und Katharine Hamnett unterstützen das aktuelle Projekt und entwarfen exklusive Drucke für eine T-Shirt-Kollektion aus organischer und Fair-Trade-Baumwolle. Über 20 Topmodels waren sich nicht zu schade und ließen sich für die gute Sache in den innovativen Shirts ablichten. Die Drucke illustrieren die Thematik Kinderarbeit, eine Kindheit mit verlorener Unschuld und Hoffnung. Sie sollen auf künstlerische Art und Weise darauf hinweisen, dass mehr als eine Millionen Kinder weltweit zu Kinderarbeit in der Baumwollproduktion gezwungen werden. Alle Verkaufserlöse der T-Shirt-Kollektion, die auf der Website der Organisation erhältlich ist, unterstützen die gemeinnützige Arbeit von EJF.

JJ ● ECO®
THE FUTURE WILL BE WHATEVER WE MAKE IT

JJ ECO
www.jackjones.com/jjeco

In 2008, Jack & Jones, one of Europe's biggest jeans manufacturers, presents its first collection made from Fair-Trade cotton. The Danish label reacts to the changing demands of the market with regard to ecological fashion, and seeks to contribute something of its own. Jack & Jones will increasingly concentrate on environmentally friendly fashion, something that can also be inferred from their new slogan, "the future will be whatever we make it." JJ ECO is a collection for fashion and environmentally conscious men. JJ ECO stands for fashion produced under human working conditions using ecological materials such as Fair-Trade cotton. This topical and stylish jeans-wear collection is available from over 600 European Jack & Jones branches. JJ ECO is a welcome addition to the ecological fashion market, not least because the jeans are available at competitive prices that do not deter potential customers from considering eco jeans.

Jack & Jones, einer der größten Jeanshersteller Europas, präsentiert seit 2008 eine Kollektion aus Fair-Trade-Baumwolle. Das dänische Label reagiert damit auf die Veränderungen des Modemarktes hinsichtlich des Themas Öko-Mode und möchte seinen eigenen Beitrag dazu leisten. So wird sich Jack & Jones in Zukunft verstärkt auf umweltfreundliche Mode konzentrieren und belegt dies nicht nur mit seinem Slogan: „The future will be whatever we make." Die Kollektion JJ ECO ist eine Linie für mode- und umweltbewusste Männer. JJ ECO steht für Mode, die unter menschenwürdigen Arbeitsbedingungen produziert und aus ökologischen Materialien, wie z.B. Fair-Trade-Baumwolle, hergestellt wird. In über 600 europäischen Jack & Jones Filialen wird diese zeitgemäße und stylische Jeanswear-Kollektion angeboten. Für den ökologischen Modemarkt ist Jack & Jones mit JJ ECO eine Bereicherung, denn die Jeans werden zu einem attraktiven Preis angeboten, so dass es für die Kunden keine Preisfrage ist, ob zu ökologischer oder normaler Jeansware gegriffen wird.

Junky Styling | Designers: Annika Sanders, Kerry Seager
Fall Winter 2008/09
www.junkystyling.co.uk

Junky Styling fashion is synonymous with top quality second-hand clothing from England. The pieces are taken apart, cut, and redesigned to produce completely new items. Also to be found are recycled or Fair-Trade clothing made from organic materials. The designers Annika Sanders and Kerry Seager also offer a repair service for clients called "wardrobe surgery", which enables them either to prolong the life of their timeless and original pieces or have them redesigned to create something completely new and different. The focus lies on individual design; no item is like another. In their creative work with old items of clothing, Junky designers follow a path of sustainability, placing great emphasis on ecologically friendly manufacturing processes. Their collections can be found in their own designer shop in London and also in independent shops in Rome, Athens, Zürich, and Stockholm.

Die Mode von Junky Styling steht für recycelte Second-Hand-Bekleidung von bester Qualität aus England. Fundstücke werden dekonstruiert, neu geschnitten und komplett in ein neues Bekleidungsstück umgewandelt. Im Junky Shop findet man recycelte, Fair-Trade oder aus organischem Material hergestellte, ökologisch gerechte Kleidung. Die Designerinnen Annika Sanders und Kerry Seager bieten ihren Kunden zudem einen Reparaturservie an, den sie „Operation Kleidung" nennen, durch den sie zeitlosen und originalen Stücken eine längere Lebensdauer ermöglichen oder in etwas ganz Neues umarbeiten. Der Fokus des Labels liegt auf individuellem Design, kein Kleidungsstück gleicht dem anderen. Die Designerinnen von Junky verhalten sich in ihrer kreativen Arbeit mit alter Kleidung nachhaltig und legen gleichzeitig großen Wert auf umweltfreundliche Herstellungsprozesse. Junky Styling bietet eine Linie für Frauen und eine für Männer an. Ihre Kollektionen sind nicht nur in ihrem eigenen Londoner Shop zu finden, sondern auch bei Einzelhändlern in Rom, Athen, Zürich und Stockholm.

Katharine E Hamnett

Spring Summer 2008
www.katharinehamnett.com

Katharine Hamnett's critique of the way the fashion world operates cannot be missed. Huge lettering adorns her T-Shirts: „NO MORE FASHION VICTIMS" or „ORGANIC COTTON CAN MAKE POVERTY HISTORY FOR 1,000,000 FARMERS". Fashion and sustainability are of primary importance to the London based designer. Katharine Hamnett has been using them as buzzwords since 1989 and she displays her lasting commitment to the environment and health through her fashion. According to the World Health Organization, some 20,000 people die annually in the cotton farming industry through accidental pesticide poisonings. 100,000 suffer from lifelong ailments. Following a label relaunch in 2005, her collections adhere to strict ethical guidelines. Katharine Hamnett produces T-shirts made of ecologically friendly pesticide-free cotton in licensed, humane factories. Fashion, according to her T-shirts, should not only give you a good feeling but also a clear conscience.

Bei Katharine Hamnett sticht die Kritik an den Arbeitsweisen der Modebranche an sich direkt ins Auge. In riesigen Buchstaben druckt sie ihre Ansichten auf T-Shirts: „NO MORE FASHION VICTIMS" oder „ORGANIC COTTON CAN MAKE POVERTY HISTORY FOR 1,000,000 FARMERS". Mode und Nachhaltigkeit sind für die Londoner Designerin von größter Bedeutung. Katharine Hamnett setzt diese Schlagworte schon seit 1989 konsequent mit einem beständigen Engagement für Umwelt und Gesundheit in ihren Kollektionen um. Laut Weltgesundheitsorganisation sterben jährlich 20.000 Menschen durch unfallbedingte Pestizidvergiftungen beim Baumwollanbau, 100.000 leiden unter lebenslangen Beschwerden. Nach einem Label-Relaunch 2005 sind ihre Kollektionen strikt an ethisch gerechte Richtlininen angelegt. Katharine Hamnett stellt ihre T-Shirts frei von Pestiziden aus Bio-Baumwolle und nur in lizensierten, sozial gerechten Fabriken her. Mode, so die Botschaft ihrer T-Shirts, soll nicht nur für ein gutes Gefühl, sondern auch für ein gutes Gewissen sorgen.

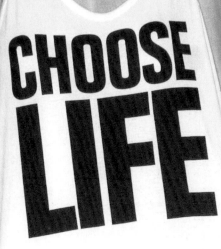

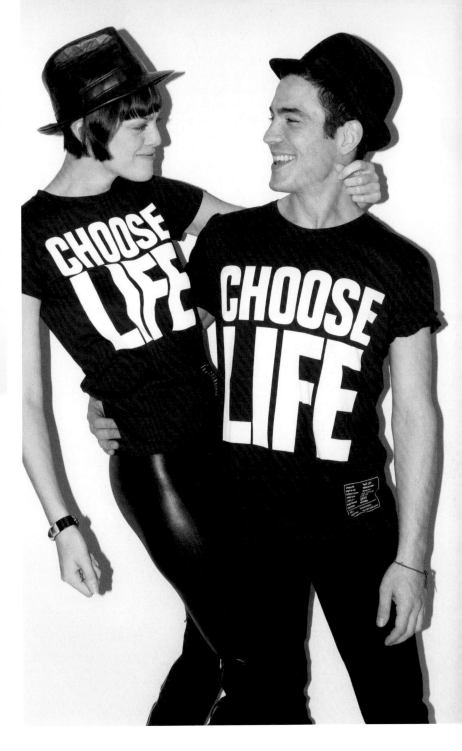

Kuyichi | CEO: Tony Tonnaer

Fall Winter 2008/09

ww.kuyichi.com

One of the first jeans labels, Kuyichi has successfully combined the concepts of cool street-wear and social responsibility. That was a step in the right direction: the innovative collections are available in more than 15 countries and 850 shops throughout the world; the outlook is bullish. The ambition to establish organic cotton and fair trade jeans on the market led to the 2001 foundation of this label by the Dutch non governemental organization Solidaridad in collaboration with experts from the fashion industry. Kuyichi works with factories in Turkey, Tunisia, and India, who commit themselves—largely voluntarily—to humane working conditions and pay controls. Between 60% and 70% of the products are made from pesticide-free cotton, thus not harming plantation workers. Kuyichi's philosophy can be inferred from its logo: the circle symbolizes the earth, the plus stands for positive. The label seeks to benefit both nature and humanity and to create an overall awareness of ethically correct fashion.

Kuyichi ist es als einer der ersten Jeans-Marken erfolgreich gelungen, lässige Streetwear ohne den Verzicht auf soziale Verantwortung zu entwickeln. Das Vertrauen hat sich bewährt: Die innovativen Kollektionen sind heute weltweit mit stark steigender Tendenz in mehr als 15 Ländern und 850 Läden erhältlich. Mit der Ambition, organische Baumwolle und Fair Trade Jeans auf dem Markt zu etablieren, wurde das niederländische Unternehmen im Jahr 2001 von der autonomen Hilfsorganisation Solidaridad in Kollaboration mit Experten aus der Modebranche ins Leben gerufen. Kuyichi arbeitet mit Produktionsstätten in der Türkei, Tunesien und Indien, die sich zum größten Teil freiwillig unabhängigen Kontrollen unterziehen. Hier wird geprüft, ob sie bestimmte Standards wie Mindestlöhne und würdige Arbeitsbedingungen einhalten. 60% bis 70% aller Produkte sind aus Baumwolle gefertigt, die nicht mit Pestiziden behandelt wurde und somit auch nicht gesundheitsschädlich für die Arbeiter auf den Baumwollfeldern ist. Die Philosophie von Kuyichi symbolisiert das Logo: der Kreis steht für die Erde, das Plus-Zeichen für das Positive. Das Label will dem Menschen und der Natur Gutes tun und auch bei anderen ein Bewusstsein für ethisch korrekte Mode schaffen.

Levi's | Designer: You Nguyen

Fall Winter 2008/09

www.levi.com

The inventor of jeans recently came out with its first sustainable model. The production of eco jeans is based on a carefully organized system, including health and safety issues as well as conservation and social responsibility. Eco jeans are made of 100% organic cotton and other sustainable product components such as natural coconut husks and non-galvanized metal buttons. Traditional rivets are replaced by sturdy quilting seams. In its drive for sustainable development, the Levi's team has come up with an innovative and chemical-free production process, which makes use of environmentally friendly additives such as indigo or potato starch. The jeans received the EKO Sustainable Textile award from the Control Union World Group, which is the world's leading test and certification center for sustainable manufacturing and products. Levi's eco jeans are further proof that creative product development and a value chain dependent on sustainable raw materials and production processes are not mutually exclusive.

Der Erfinder der Jeanshose brachte vor kurzem seine erste nachhaltige Jeans auf den Markt. Levi's legt bei der Produktion der Eco Jeans Wert auf einen minutiös durchorganisierten Systemplan, auch im Hinblick auf die Bereiche Gesundheit und Sicherheit, Umweltschutz und soziale Verantwortung. Die Eco Jeans bestehen aus 100% organischer Baumwolle und weiteren nachhaltigen Produktkomponenten wie natürliche Kokosschale und nicht galvanisierte Metallknöpfe. Die traditionellen Nieten werden durch stabile Steppnähte ersetzt. In seinem intensiven Bemühen im Bereich nachhaltiger Entwicklung hat das Levi's Team einen innovativen und chemikalienfreien Verarbeitungsprozess entwickelt, bei dem ausschließlich umweltfreundliche Zusätze wie natürliches Indigo oder Kartoffelstärke verwendet werden. Die Jeans wurden mit dem Gütezeichen „EKO Sustainable Textile" ausgezeichnet, eine Zertifizierung von Control Union Certifications, der weltweit führenden Prüfungs- und Zertifizierungsstelle für nachhaltige Produktion und Produkte. Levi's Eco Jeans sind ein weiterer Beweis dafür, dass sich kreative Produktentwicklung und eine Wertschöpfungskette, in die nachhaltige Rohstoffe und Herstellungsprozesse integriert sind, gegenseitig nicht ausschließen.

MORE
TREES
PLEASE

Misericordia | CEO: Aurelyen Conty
Fall Winter 2008/09
www.misionmisericordia.com

The Peruvian fashion label Misericordia combines Fair-Trade and development aid with design and individuality. Misericordia stands for charity, and this word describes Mathieu Reumaux and Aurelyen Conty, the owner, perfectly. The two Frenchmen were traveling through Peru and stopped over in Ventanilla, where the local school uniform caught their eye. The so-called Misericordia tracksuits were made by the pupils of the Misericordia school themselves. The two Europeans started helping the village by selling their products in Europe. Today collections are designed with minor modifications and in collaboration with famous designers such as Bernhard Wilhelm. The company's own workshop in Lima with a staff of 32 produces the apparel, and concept stores world-wide market the collections. Collections consist of hand-made limited editions made from 100% Peruvian raw materials. 80% of the T-shirts are made from organic cotton. All revenues go directly to the project and are used to improve the local socio-economic structure, guarantee fair pay, more jobs, and education. Misericordia places great emphasis on humane and environmentally friendly production practices as well as raising awareness in industrial nations for the further support of sustainable development aid.

Das peruanische Fashion-Label Misericordia vereint die Begriffe Fair-Trade und Entwicklungshilfe mit Design und Individualität. Misericordia steht für Barmherzigkeit und dieses Wort beschreibt gleichzeitig Mathieu Reumaux und Aurelyen Conty, den heutigen Firmenbesitzer. Die beiden Franzosen kamen auf ihrer Reise durch Peru nach Ventanilla und waren begeistert von der dortigen Schuluniform, der Misericordia Tracksuits, die Schüler der gleichnamigen Schule selbst nähten. Sie begannen der Dorfgemeinschaft durch den Vertrieb ihrer Produkte in Europa zu helfen. Mit leichten Modifikationen im Design und der Zusammenarbeit mit namhaften Designern wie Bernhard Wilhelm entstehen heute in einer eigenen Werkstatt mit 32 Mitarbeitern in Lima Kollektionen, die inzwischen über Concept-Stores weltweit verkauft werden. Die Kollektionen werden in limitierter Auflage von Hand hergestellt und bestehen zu 100% aus peruanischen Rohstoffen. 80% der T-Shirts sind bereits aus organischer Baumwolle. Alle Verkaufserlöse fließen direkt zurück in das Projekt und dienen dem Aufbau sozial-ökonomischer Strukturen vor Ort, gewährleisten eine faire Bezahlung, weitere Arbeitsplätze und Ausbildung. Misericordia legt Wert auf eine die Menschenrechte achtende, umweltgerechte Produktion und letztendlich auch darauf, das Bewusstsein in den Industrienationen für die weitere Unterstützung nachhaltiger Entwicklungshilfeprojekte zu schärfen.

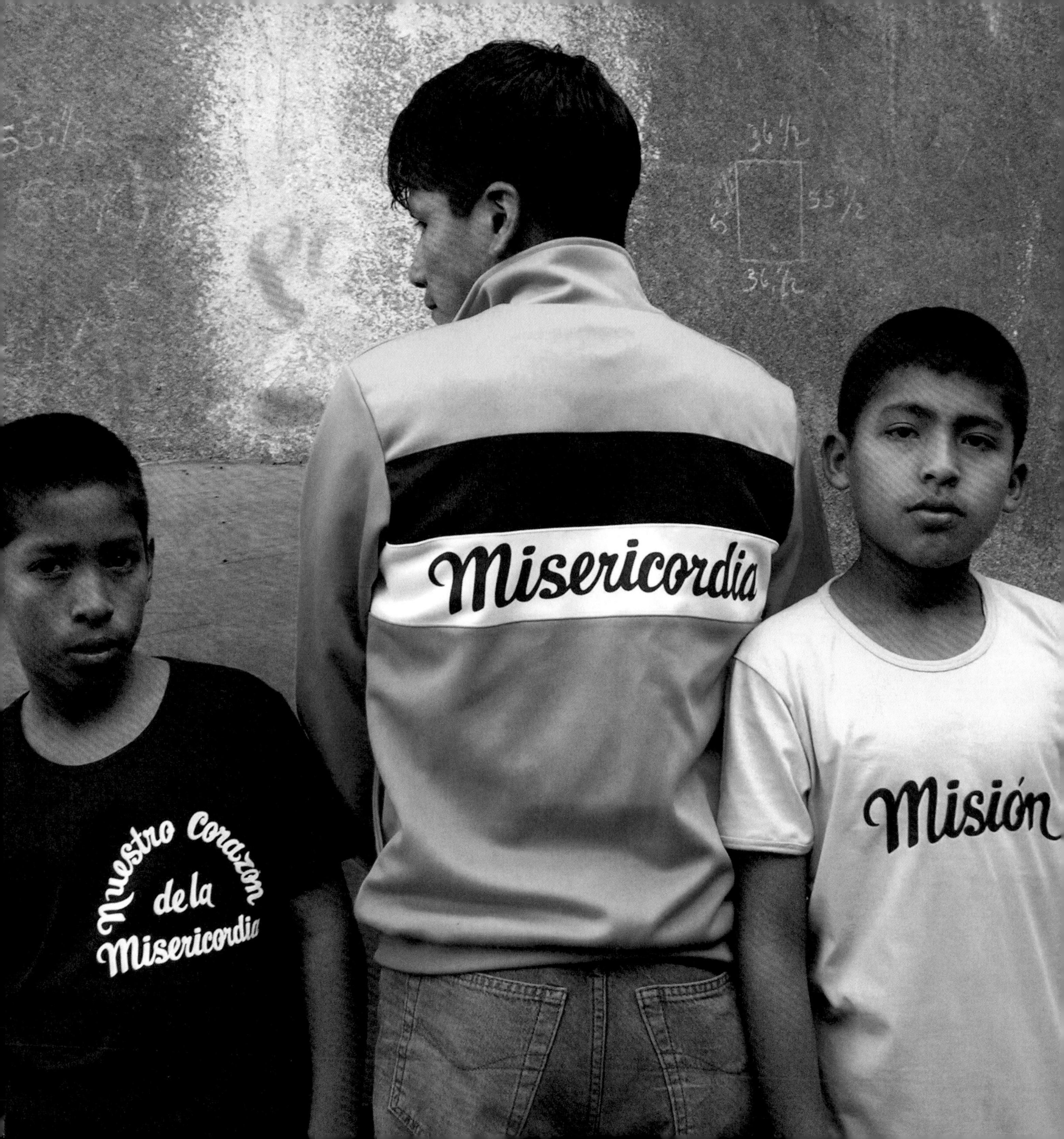
Misericordia
Misión
Nuestro Corazón
de la
Misericordia

OLOGY | Designer: Lorena Santin-Andrade

Spring Summer 2008

www.cgology.ca

The Canadian label COTTON GINNY expanded its collection in 2006 to include the eco-aware organic line OLOGY. The label produces fashion from 100% certified organic cotton. Lorena Santin-Andrade, fashion designer and creative chief at OLOGY, infuses the company culture with social and environmental responsibility. Its mainstay is organically produced bio-cotton. Inspired by African, Indian, and Australian production processes, OLOGY manufactures innovative fabrics using such unusual raw materials as milk, soy, bamboo, corn, and jade. The resulting collections are therefore not only exotic and ecologically sound but also boast special properties: corn production processes make the materials fire retardant, milk makes materials breathe better, and a special process using pearls has materials afford natural UV protection.

Im Jahr 2006 erweiterte das kanadische Label COTTON GINNY sein Angebot mit der ökologisch bewussten und organischen Linie OLOGY. Das Label produziert Mode aus 100% zertifizierter Bio-Baumwolle. Als Modedesignerin und Kreativ-Chefin von OLOGY integriert Lorena Santin-Andrade die soziale Verantwortung gegenüber der Umwelt mit in das Unternehmen. Dabei spielen Bio-Baumwolle und organisch hergestellte Baumwolle die Hauptrolle. Inspiriert von Verarbeitungstechniken aus Afrika, Indien und Australien stellt OLOGY innovative Stoffe mit außergewöhnlichen Ausgangsmaterialien wie z.B. Milch, Soja, Bambus, Mais und Jade her. Dadurch erhalten die Kollektionen nicht nur einen exotischen und umweltfreundlichen Charakter, sondern die Stoffe zudem besondere Materialeigenschaften: Verarbeitungstechniken mit Mais machen Materialien feuerresistent, Milch macht die Stoffe besonders atmungsaktiv und durch ein spezielles Verfahren, in dem Perlen verarbeitet werden, erhalten die Stoffe einen natürlichen UV-Schutz.

Nike

Spring Summer 2008
www.nikeresponsibility.com

For over 10 years now, the "Nike Considered" philosophy has targeted sustainable production and sought solutions to minimize environmental pollution. The "considered" approach starts with the design and carries through to (but does not stop at) production, because it takes account of the environmental impact of all decisions, whether this concerns material procurement, waste management, or packaging. All Nike "considered" products are manufactured according to these environmentally sound principles and using environmentally friendly materials. Apart from this eco-friendly product line, Nike is also introducing recycling for sports shoes. Instead of being burned, used sneakers, trainers, or manufacturing waste and remnants can be recycled to create new flooring materials for sports venues. The brand "Nike-Grind" uses these recycled materials to create a number of raw materials, such as recycled rubber or rubber foam, which are used in the production of racetracks or indoor basketball courts. Since Nike's introduction of the Refuse-A-Shoe program in the USA in 1993, more than 20 million worn out trainers have provided flooring materials for over 250 donated sports fields!

Seit über 10 Jahren fokussiert Nike's sogenannte Considered-Philosophie eine nachhaltige Produktion und strebt nach Lösungen für eine geringere Umweltbelastung. Der Considered-Ansatz beginnt beim Entwurf und geht weit über die Produktion hinaus. Denn Nike Considered berücksichtigt die Auswirkungen aller Entscheidungen auf die Umwelt, bei Materialbeschaffung und Abfallmanagement ebenso wie bei der Verpackung. Alle Produkte der Nike Considered-Linie werden nach umweltschonenden Methoden und aus umweltfreundlichem Material gefertigt. Neben dieser umweltfreundlichen Produktreihe führte Nike ein Recycling für Sportschuhe ein. Anstatt auf dem Müll verbrannt zu werden, können gebrauchte Sneaker und Turnschuhe, Reste aus der Schuhherstellung und Ausschussware als Rohstoff für Sportböden verwertet werden. Aus den recycelten Materialien wird unter der Marke „Nike-Grind" eine Reihe von Werkstoffen wie Recyclinggummi und Schaumstoff produziert, die z.B. Verwendung bei der Herstellung von Laufbahnen oder Indoor-Basketballplätzen finden. Seitdem das Nike Refuse-A-Shoe Programm 1993 zuerst in den USA eingeführt wurde, sind mehr als 20 Millionen abgetragene Sportschuhe im Recycling-Programm gelandet, die über 250 gestifteten Sportplätzen den Boden lieferten!

Skunkfunk | Designer: Mikel Feijoo
Fall Winter 2008/09
www.skunkfunk.com

Organic cotton + ethically traded + carbon neutral manufacturing = 100% sustainable = 100% earth positive—that is the equation of the Basque street-wear label Skunkfunk, placing it firmly among the eco trend designer labels. Bamboo and soy mixtures are the basis of high-quality, environmentally friendly materials for the Skunkfunk collection of shirts, tops, sweaters, and trousers. Production, too, adheres to environmentally friendly procedures. The label follows earth-positive guidelines, which make almost exclusive use of sustainable energy resources such as wind and solar power and guarantee organic and ethically correct farming methods. Skunkfunk leads the way not only in fashion and urban style but also when it comes to the new green revolution within the fashion industry. Skunkfunk understands fashion as a way to express a certain lifestyle and strives to translate this into its designs. The company's commitment to ecological awareness clearly a very positive step, because there can be no doubt that Skunkfunk's young target audience will be increasingly confronted with environmental problems.

Organic Cotton + Ethically Traded + Carbon Neutral manufacturing = 100% Sustainable = 100% Earth Positive, so lautet die Formel des baskischen Streetwear-Label Skunkfunk. Das Label liegt damit voll im Green-Design Trend. Bambus- und Sojamischungen bilden die Basis für die hochwertigen, umweltfreundlichen Stoffe ihrer Skunkfunk Natural Clothes Kollektion, bestehend aus Shirts, Tops, Sweater und Hosen. Auch in der Produktion zeigen sich Skunkfunk umweltbewusst. Das Label richtet sich nach den Earth-Positive-Leitlinien, bei denen fast ausschließlich mit erneuerbaren Energien wie Wind und Solar gearbeitet wird. Zudem ist dabei ein biologischer Anbau unter ethischen Gesichtspunkten garantiert. Skunkfunk ist nicht nur in Sachen Mode und Urban-Style Trend, sondern zählt zu einem der Vorreiter der Grünen Revolution in der Bekleidungsindustrie. Skunkfunk versteht Mode als Mittel zum Ausdruck eines bestimmten Lifestyles. Sie versuchen in ihrem Design, die Bedürfnisse in Trend zu übersetzen. So ist ihr Engagement für ein ökologisches Bewusstsein absolut positiv zu bewerten, da Skunkfunk eine junge Zielgruppe anspricht, die sich mit Sicherheit verstärkt mit Umweltproblematiken auseinandersetzen muss.

Smiley Collection | CEO: Nicolas Loufrani

Fall Winter 2008/09 (page 131), Spring Summer 2008 (pages 132-133)

www.smileycollection.net

Who does not remember the smiley logo from way back? A hippie symbol of love, peace and happiness during the 1970s, part of London's underground rave scene of the 1980s, and from the 90s an integral part of emails and text messages from billions of people throughout the world. As of Fall 2007 smiley is back! Under the management of Nicolas Loufrani, son of smiley inventor and executive of Smileyworld Limited, the label has declared its aim to make the world smile. However, the company is not only after its customers' lust for life and fun. It is also after a responsible way of treating the environment and ethically sound action. These include 100 percent organic cotton for the fall and winter collections 2008/2009, Fair-Trade, adherence to ethical standards such as fair working conditions, no to child labor or animal experiments, fair wages and environmentally friendly measures. 10% of the proceeds go the SOS group, a charity that supports victims of social exclusion. Smiley collection combines fun, charity, and social responsibility to humanity and nature—in the words of its motto, "share your smile with those in need!"

Wer kennt das Smiley-Logo nicht noch aus alten Kindertagen? In den 70ern ein Symbol der Hippie-Bewegung für „Love, Peace & Happiness", in den 80ern Teil des Londoner Rave Undergrounds und seit den 90ern schließlich fester Bestandteil von E-Mail- & SMS-Kommunikation von Milliarden von Menschen auf der ganzen Welt. Seit Herbst 2007 ist der Smiley wieder zurück! Unter der Führung von Nicolas Loufrani, dem Sohn des Smiley-Erfinders und Geschäftsführer der Smileyworld Limited, hat es sich die Marke zum Ziel gesetzt, ein Lächeln in die Welt zu transportieren. Nicht nur die Lebensfreude und der Spaß seiner Träger ist dem Label wichtig, sondern auch ein verantwortungsvoller Umgang mit der Umwelt und ethisches Handeln. Dazu zählen die mit der Herbst/Winter 2008/2009 Kollektion zu 100% verwendeter Bio-Baumwolle, Fair-Trade, die Einhaltung ethischer Standards wie z.B. gerechten Arbeitsbedingungen, die Absage an Kinderarbeit oder Tierversuche, eine faire Lohnzahlungspraxis und umweltfreundliche Maßnahmen. 10% der Erlöse gehen an die SOS Group, die die Opfer sozialer Ausgrenzung unterstützt. Smiley Collection vereint Spaß, Charity und soziale Verantwortung gegenüber Mensch und Natur – ganz nach dem Motto: „Share your smile with those in need!"

NO NUKES

Smiley®
collection

Smiley

Smiley World Association
Share your smile with those in need
www.smileyworldassociation.org

SMILEY UNIVERSITY

100% ORGANIC COTTON

American Apparel | CEO: Dov Charney

Fall Winter 2008/09

www.americanapparel.net

American Apparel has proven that ecologically and socio-politically sound fashion can be sexy and modern. According to the company, production does not take place in sweatshops, i.e. the label does not employ underpaid seamstresses working in inhumane conditions in the third world. The origins of their materials are not known nor are their suppliers. But instead of outsourcing everything, production and marketing are all handled from the base in Los Angeles. Working conditions include paid leisure time, health care, subsidized meals, and English language courses. The American Apparel Organic Cotton collection is a selection of best selling designs produced from 100% certified organically grown cotton with lower use of pesticides. Although customers will not find a great selection of this eco-line in any of the AA shops yet, the label aims to use organic cotton for its main collection. The L.A. T-shirt factory is proof that politically correct fashion does make money: the company with its 8500 staff has doubled its turnover to 350 million dollars in only four years and has become one of America's largest manufacturers of T-shirts.

American Apparel hat bewiesen, dass Mode, die umwelt- und sozialverträglich entstanden ist, sexy und modern sein kann. Das Label produziert laut Unternehmensdarstellung nicht in Sweatshops, lässt also keine unterbezahlten Näherinnen in den „Schwitzbuden" der Dritten Welt für sich nähen. Die Herkunft von Materialien von Zulieferern sind nicht bekannt. Statt kostengünstigem Outsourcing finden neben der Produktion auch der Vertrieb und das Marketing unter einem Dach in Los Angeles statt. Die dort Angestellten erhalten bezahlte Freizeit, eine Gesundheitsvorsorge, subventionierte Verpflegung und Unterricht in Englisch als Fremdsprache. American Apparels Organic Cotton Kollektion ist eine Selektion der beliebtesten Kollektionsteile und besteht zu 100% aus zertifizierter organischer Baumwolle, die mit weniger Pestizideinsatz hergestellt wurde. Obwohl man bis heute in den AA-Läden nur einige wenige Shirts dieser noch sehr kleinen Öko-Linie findet, ist es Ziel, nach und nach organische Baumwolle auch in die Hauptkollektionen mit aufzunehmen. Die T-Shirt Fabrik aus L. A. ist ein Beweis dafür, dass man mit politisch korrekter Mode auch Geld verdienen kann: Das Unternehmen beschäftigt weltweit derzeit 8.500 Mitarbeiter und hat seinen Umsatz innerhalb von vier Jahren auf 350 Millionen Dollar verdoppelt und ist mittlerweile einer der größten T-Shirt-Produzenten in Amerika.

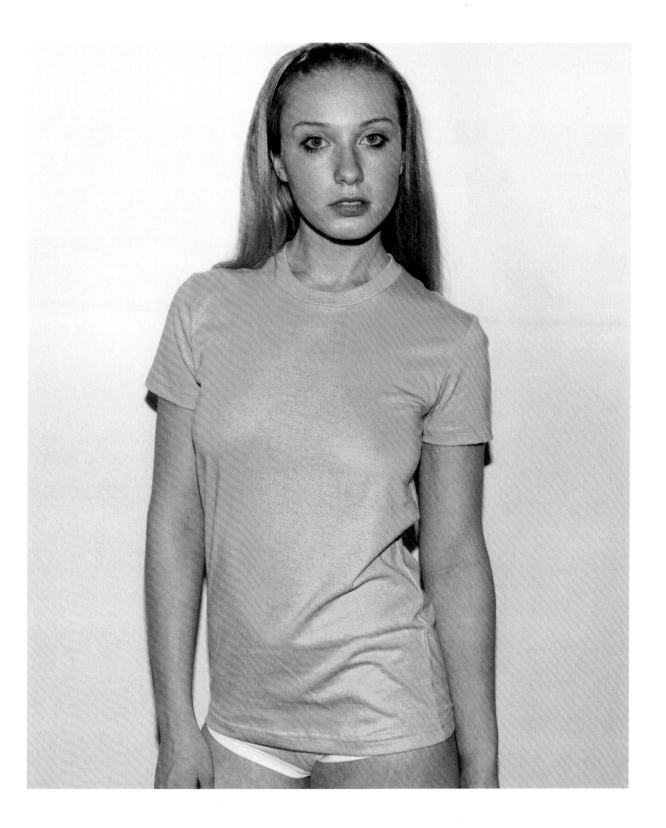

BEAU SOLEIL | Designer: Anne Salvatore Epstein

Fall Winter 2008/09

ww.shopbeausoleil.com

Anne Salvatore Epstein's eco friendly collection BEAU SOLEIL unquestionably belongs to the ever growing trend of "green design". BEAU SOLEIL, named after the designer's favorite oyster, is built around the values of sustainability, Fair-Trade, humane working conditions for manufacturers, and organic materials. The label offers its clients modern, environmentally friendly fashion without pesticides. It was when the designer became pregnant, that she and her husband transformed their way of thinking. They left their abundant New York lifestyle for a modern, organic, and simple way of life. They applied the same ethically correct principles to their fashion collections. Epstein uses materials such as bamboo, sustainable fabrics, eco cotton dyed with vegetable based dyes, and tencel (which is extracted from eucalyptus trees), vintage materials, recycled remnants, and leather remnants from other manufacturers.

Anne Salvatore Epstein's öko-freundliche Kollektion BEAU SOLEIL liegt voll im "Green Designed"-Trend. BEAU SOLEIL, bennant nach der Lieblingsauster der Designerin, setzt seine Schwerpunkte auf Nachhaltigkeit, Fair-Trade, sozial gerechte Arbeitsbedingungen für die Hersteller und organische Materialien. Deswegen kann das Label seinen Kunden umweltfreundliche und schadstofffreie Kleidung anbieten ohne dabei auf Modernität verzichten zu müssen. Als die Designerin schwanger wurde, trat bei ihr und ihrem Mann ein Sinn- und Lebenswandel ein. Die beiden tauschten ihren überschwenglichen New Yorker Lebensstil gegen eine moderne, organische und einfache Art zu leben. Diese ethisch korrekte Art übernahm sie auch für ihre Modekollektionen. Epstein verwendet heute für ihre Kollektionen Materialien aus Bambus, nachhaltige Stoffe, pflanzlich gefärbte, organische Baumwolle und Tencel, das aus Eukalyptusbäumen gewonnen wird. Zudem verarbeitet sie Vintagematerialien, recycelte Ausschussware und Lederreste anderer Produzenten.

Filippa K | Filippa Knutson

Fall Winter 2008/09
www.filippa-k.com

The Swedish fashion label Filippa K has come out with a small, ecologically correct line of T-shirts, which has received the "Nordic Ecolabel" stamp of environmentally friendly approval. Nordic Ecolabel is an independent, charitable organization. The company emblem, the swan, demonstrates that the products were tested according to ecological standards and found to be environmentally friendly. Nordic Ecolabel controls the entire manufacturing process, starting with cotton farming right through to the production of the finished article. Filippa K's eco collection is comprised of just two women's and two men's T-shirts. With this small, sustainable line Filippa K seeks to lay down a marker and signal its start in the world of long-term environmentally friendly thinking and sustainable design. Although the T-Shirt line is very small, Filippa K manages to increase awareness of ecologically sound fashion because, with its 750 shops in Europe, North America, and Australia, the brand is one of Sweden's fastest growing fashion labels, which convinces with its timeless, yet modern designs.

Auch das schwedische Modelabel Filippa K präsentiert seit kurzem eine kleine, ökologisch gerechte T-Shirt Linie, die von der unabhängigen, gemeinnützigen Organisation „Nordic Ecolabel" als umweltfreundlich anerkannt wurde. Der Schwan, deren offizielles Zeichen, demonstriert, dass das damit ausgezeichnete Produkt nach ökologischen Standards geprüft und für umweltfreundlich befunden wurde. Das Nordic Ecolabel kontrolliert den kompletten Herstellungsablauf des jeweils zu bewertenden Produkts, vom Baumwollanbau bis hin zur Produktion und dem fertigen Teil. Die Eco-Kollektion von Filippa K umfasst gerade mal zwei T-Shirts für Frauen und zwei für Herren. Mit dieser kleinen, nachhaltigen Linie will Filippa K ein Zeichen und zugleich den Startschuss für ein langfristiges, umweltfreundliches Denken und nachhaltiges Design setzen. Obwohl die T-Shirt-Linie wirklich klein ist, schafft es Filippa K damit trotzdem, ein weit verbreitetes Bewusstsein für ökologisch gerechte Mode zu schaffen. Denn Filippa K ist mit derzeit 750 Shops in Europa, Nordamerika und Australien eine der schnellst wachsenden schwedischen Modefirmen, die mit zeitlosem modernen Design überzeugt.

FROM SOMEWHERE | Designer: Orsola de Castro

Fall Winter 2008/09

www.fromsomewhere.co.uk

FROM SOMEWHERE started transforming vintage clothes in 1997 by including innovative details. It was one of the first fashion brands to make the headlines because it utilized old textiles. FROM SOMEWHERE addresses the question of what happens to fashion industry waste such as remnants, swatches, and deficient goods. The answer is simple: they land in the trash. This makes the fashion industry—not to mention its production process—one of the worst polluters around. FROM SOMEWHERE's collections consist 100% of these vintage materials that were to end up in the waste bin—yet they are still beautiful and functional. Each garment is made of individually recycled textiles such as cashmere, cotton, silk, jersey, tweed or knits. Designer Orsola de Castro creates her special knits from waste collected specially for her from different italian fashion houses. The designer gives the items (often rejected for a single small weaving irregularity) a new lease of life and transforms them into new and stunning creations.

1997 begann FROM SOMEWHERE damit Vintage Ware zu transformieren und mit innovativen Details aufzuwerten. Damit gehört die Marke zu einer der ersten in der Modewelt, die mit der Verwertung alter Textilien Furore machten. FROM SOMEWHERE stellt sich die Frage, was mit den Abfällen der Modeindustrie wie zum Beispiel Stoffresten, Musterteilen, fehlerhafter Ware, nach dem Abschluss einer Produktionsreihe passiert. Sie landen im Müll. Das macht die Modeindus-trie – abgesehen von der Produktion – zu einer der umweltverschmutzensten Branchen überhaupt. FROM SOMEWHERE's Kollektionen bestehen zu 100% aus diesen „Vintage- und Abfallmaterialien", die nicht gebraucht wurden, aber trotzdem noch wunderschön und funktionell sind. Jedes Teil stammt individuell aus wiedergewonnenen Textilien wie Kaschmir, Baumwolle, Seide, Jersey, Tweed oder Strickwaren. Die Designerin Orsola de Castro gewinnt ihre besonderen Strickwaren aus der für sie gesammelten Ausschusswaren von verschiedenen italienischen Modefirmen. Den oft nur wegen eines einzigen Webfehlers aussortierten Stücken verleiht die Designerin ein neues Leben und verwandelt sie in neue, wunderschöne Kreationen.

Izzy Lane | Designer: Isobel Davies

Fall Winter 2008/09

www.izzylane.co.uk

Designer Isobel Davies' love for top quality clothing, animals, and her native Britain culminated in the label Izzy Lane. It makes extensive use of wool from Shetland and Wensleydale sheep. Activist Davies saves the sheep from the slaughterhouse and is even prepared to pay over the odds for them. The animals are then free to graze on their own field and supply her with the bulk of material for her collection. A staunch vegetarian, Isobel Davies uses Izzy Lane to present an economic model that allows sheep to live a normal life without ending up on a plate. The label takes a firm stand against both animal abuse and wool imports to Britain —a country which once was a major wool exporter itself. Isobel Davies started producing her own wool in 2002. Today she provides work for the last of 51 worsted spinners and one of the few dyers left in the country. The knitwear is produced by old machines dating back to Queen Victoria. Izzy Lane's clients can be 100% sure that the products are both ecologically and socio-politically sound. After all, the designer is able to oversee and control production process from the raw material, i.e. the sheep, through manufacturing all the way to the finished product.

Die Entwürfe des Labels Izzy Lane sind das Ergebnis der Liebe seiner Designerin Isobel Davies für hochwertige Kleidung, Tiere und ihr Heimatland Großbritannien. Das Label verarbeitet vor allem Wolle von Shetland und Wensleydale Schafen. Die Aktivistin Davies rettet die Schafe vor dem Schlachter und bezahlt für sie manchmal sogar einen besseren Preis. Diese Tiere leben auf einer eigenen Weide und liefern einen Großteil der Materialien für die Kollektion. Die überzeugte Vegetarierin Isobel Davies präsentiert anhand von Izzy Lane ein ökonomisches Modell, bei dem Schafe normal existieren und aufwachsen können ohne als Mahlzeit für den Menschen enden zu müssen. Die Marke wendet sich gegen die Misshandlung von Tieren und den Import von Wolle nach Großbritannien, das Land, das einst selbst führend im Wollexport war. 2002 begann Isobel Davies damit, Wolle im eigenen Land zu produzieren. Heute beschäftigt sie den letzten von 51 Wollspinnern im Land und einen der wenigen Textilfärber. Die Strickwaren werden an alten Maschinen aus der viktorianischen Zeit gefertigt. Bei Izzy Lane kann sich der Verbraucher sicher sein, dass er 100% ökologisch und sozial gerechte Mode erhält, da die Designer ein jedes Kleidungsstück von der Wollgewinnung über den Herstellungsprozess bis hin zum Kleidungsstück im eigenen Land überschauen und kontrollieren können.

Onagono | Designer: Tomomi Kojo-Robertson

2007/08

www.onagono.com

Onagono is an ethically correct fashion label from the UK that specializes in high-quality organic materials and engages in Fair-Trade practices. The founder and designer Tomomi Kojo-Robertson, originally from Japan, knows the meaning of sustainability in fashion production. Issues such as the environment and the gap between rich and poor countries have been playing on the designer's mind to such an extent that she applied the same high standards to her designs and to her label's environmentally friendly and sustainable production processes. Onagono implemented these high demands masterfully—the company has been a Fair-Trade licensee since 2007. Clothing is made 100% from Fair-Trade cotton produced by an ISO certified manufacturer in India. Even the labels and catalogs contain more than 50% recycled materials. Onagono collections are on sale in Britain, Japan, Germany, Belgium, France, and the USA.

Onagono ist ein ethisch korrektes Mode-Label aus Großbritannien, das sich qualitativ hochwertigen, organischen Materialien und Fair-Trade-Praktiken widmet. Die Gründerin und Designerin japanischer Herkunft Tomomi Kojo-Robertson ist sich der Bedeutung von Nachhaltigkeit in der Modeproduktion bewusst. Themen wie Umwelt und die Kluft zwischen armen und reichen Ländern beschäftigte die Designerin so sehr, dass sie die hohen Maßstäbe nicht nur an ihre Entwürfe, sondern auch an eine umweltbewusste und nachhaltige Herstellung setzte. Onagono hat seine Ansprüche meisterhaft umgesetzt, denn seit 2007 ist die Firma ein Fair-Trade Lizenznehmer. Kleidungsstücke bestehen aus 100% Fair-Trade-Baumwolle und werden von einem ISO-zertifizierten Hersteller in Indien produziert. Sogar die Labeletiketten und Kataloge sind zu über 50% aus recyceltem Material hergestellt. Nicht nur in Großbritannien werden die Onagono-Kollektionen vertrieben, sondern auch in Japan, Deutschland, Belgien, Frankreich, den Niederlanden und den USA.

Popomomo | Designer: Lizz Wassermann
Spring Summer 2008/09
www.popomomo.com

At a time when fashion is not necessarily original, but is often wasteful, the American fashion label Popomomo concentrates on new and true items of clothing. Popomomo is against "disposable fashion" and calls for sustainable, innovative designs. To that end, designer Lizz Wassermann creates simple cuts to create complex shapes, which are intellectual, sexy, and self-confident. She always uses organic and sustainable materials and low impact dyes for collections and ensures that her domestic suppliers use sustainable production methods. Pompomomo looks to strenghten its ecological aspects of the line through eco-shipping, and eco-energy.

In einer Zeit, in der Mode nicht immer unbedingt originell, aber oft verschwenderisch ist, möchte das amerikanische Label Popomomo nur Mode auf den Markt bringen, die einzigartig und neu sind. Popomomo wendet sich gegen die „Einweg-Mode" und fordert langlebiges, innovatives Design. Dafür erarbeitet die Designerin Lizz Wassermann einfache Schnitte und schafft somit komplexe Formen, die intellektuell, sexy und selbstbewusst sind. Für ihre Kollektionen verwendet sie rein organische und nachhaltige Materialien. Für Färben, Drucken und Waschungen kommen natürliche Färbemittel auf umweltfreundlicher Basis zum Einsatz. Dabei achtet die Designerin stets auf eine nachhaltige Produktion im Inland. Überdies plant Popomomo die ökologischen Aspekte im ganzen Produktionskreislauf zu verstärken. Lizz Wassermann will immer mehr auf umweltfreundliche Transportmöglichkeiten und natürliche Energiequellen zurückgreifen.

room to roam | Designer: Akela Stoklas

Spring Summer 2009
www.room-to-roam.com

room to roam is a new breath of freedom that is enriching the world of eco fashion. The fashion label designs and produces organic fashion, combining fresh design with sustainability. Fashion designer Akela Stoklas describes her collection as a "new organic luxury for each and every day". room to roam stands for the desire for space and creativity, elbowroom, and the sense for untouched nature. This is the reason why room to roam collections are about endangered landscapes, while each individual style surprises with exciting details and its multitude of applications. For her summer collection 2008 the designer found inspiration in the Florida Everglades. Akel Stoklas demonstrates with her label the possibilities of sustainable materials. Her exclusive mix of textiles includes denim, linen, new wool, cotton-jersey, silk, and naturally tanned leather. Every style surprises with its exciting details and its manifold diversity. Room to roam produces its fashion solely in Germany. That way the label not only guarantees highest quality but also protects the environment by eliminating long distance haulage. At the same time it helps to keep German textile workshops alive.

room to roam heißt der neue Hauch von Freiheit, der durch die grüne Modeszene weht. Das Modelabel entwirft und produziert Organic Fashion, die frisches Design und Nachhaltigkeit miteinander vereint. Die Modedesignerin Akela Stoklas beschreibt ihre Kollektionen als „neuen organischen Luxus für jeden Tag". room to roam steht für ihre Sehnsucht nach Raum für Kreativität, Bewegungsfreiheit und den Sinn für die ursprüngliche Natur. Jede room to roam Kollektion beschäftigt sich mit einer Naturlandschaft, die in ihrem Bestand gefährdet ist. Für ihre Sommerkollektion 2008 ließ sich die Designerin z.B. von den Everglades in Florida inspirieren. Mit ihrem Label zeigt Akela Stoklas, was heute bereits mit Stoffen aus nachhaltiger Herstellung möglich ist. Im exklusiven Materialmix finden sich Denim, Leinen, Schurwolle, Baumwoll-Jersey, Seide und natürlich gegerbtes Leder. Zugleich überrascht jeder einzelne Style mit spannenden Details und vielfältiger Wandelbarkeit. Gefertigt wird die Mode von room to roam ausschließlich in Deutschland. Damit sichert das Label nicht nur höchste Qualitätsansprüche in der Herstellung, sondern schont auch die Umwelt durch kurze Transportwege bei der Produktion und trägt gleichzeitig zur Erhaltung des deutschen Textilhandwerks bei.

Caloli | Designers: Carole Dichampt, Bi Zheng Qing

Fall Winter 2008/09

www.caloli.com

French fashion designer Carole Dichampt and the Chinese artist Zheng Qing developed the label Caloli. The two create hand-made masterpieces —eco-couture to be more precise—which are socio-politically correct. The design combines Chinese handicraft skills and traditional French design. Seamstress from Chinese minority groups such as the Miao and the Buyei produce for Caloli. Their wages enable them to improve local living standards and keep their villages alive. Caloli pays fair wages, thus building a lasting partnership with local producers. The designers also pay up front, so that the seamstresses do not get into debt. Caloli supports traditional Chinese handicraft skills and uses old costumes and garments for inspiration. The results are innovative designs such as a skirt with 1000 pleats or garments with complex embroidery on silk fabrics interwoven with strands of silver.

Die französische Modedesignerin Carole Dichampt entwickelte zusammen mit dem chinesischen Künstler Zheng Qing das Label Caloli. Die beiden Kreativen präsentieren heute handgeschneiderte Meisterstücke, sprich innovative Eco-Couture mit sozial gerechtem Hintergrund. Die Designerin vereint Handarbeit aus China mit französischem, traditionsreichen Designverständnis. Caloli lässt seine Kollektionen von Näherinnen, die den chinesischen Minderheiten Miao und Buyei angehören, fertigen. Durch ihren Verdienst können diese Frauen vor Ort ihre Lebensbedingungen verbessern und das Leben in den Dörfern aufrechterhalten. Caloli zahlt gerechte Löhne und setzt somit auf eine andauernde Partnerschaft mit den Produktionstätten vor Ort. Zudem leisten die Designer einen Kostenvorschuss, um eine Verschuldung der Partner zu vermeiden. Caloli unterstützt die traditionellen, handwerklichen Fähigkeiten der Näherinnen in China und lässt sich von den alten Kleidungsstilen der Völker inspirieren. Dadurch entstanden innovative Entwürfe wie ein Rock aus 1000 Falten oder Kleider mit aufwändigen Stickereien auf Seidenstoffen und mit darin verarbeiteten Silberfäden.

Céline Faizant

Fall Winter 2008/09

www.celinefaizant.fr

The French designer Céline Faizant started her career in large design houses such as Chanel and Chistian Lacroix. She began with her own line on handicraft markets on the French Riviera. She now boasts her own label and designs neither haute couture nor Prêt-à-Porter clothing. Instead she calls it "nouvelle couture". Small French workshops with considerable expertise produce her limited series of extraordinary and unique pieces. Céline Faizant makes exclusive use of ecological materials such as linen, hemp, cotton, or silk, which are either "Ecocert" or "SKAL" certified. The designer banks on transparency! Each piece of clothing comes with an "identity card" giving details of the materials' origins, manufacturing process, and working techniques applied. Céline Faizant stands for elegance based on ecological and just standards. So far, her work is only available in France.

Die französische Designerin Céline Faizant begann ihre Karriere bei großen Designerhäusern wie Chanel und Christian Lacroix. Mit ihrer eigenen Linie startete sie zuerst auf Handwerksmärkten an der französischen Riviera. Nun hat sie ihr eigenes Label – sie entwirft weder Haute Couture noch Prêt-à-Porter, ihr Design nennt sie selbst „Nouvelle Couture". Kleine französische Werkstätten, die ein umfassendes handwerkliches Wissen besitzen, fertigen die kleinen Serien von außergewöhnlichen Einzelstücken. Für ihre Kollektionen verwendet Céline Faizant ausschließlich ökologische Materialien wie Leinen, Hanf, Baumwolle oder Seide. Diese sind unter anderem zertifiziert mit „Ecocert" oder „SKAL". Transparenz wird bei Céline Faizant groß geschrieben! Jedem einzelnen Bekleidungsstück liegt ein sogenannter „Ausweis" bei, auf welchem Materialherkunft, Herstellungsprozess und Arbeitstechnik detailliert beschrieben werden. Céline Faizant steht für Eleganz auf ökologischer und gerechter Basis. Bisher wird ihre Mode ausschließlich in Frankreich vertrieben.

LINDA LOUDERMILK

Linda Loudermilk

Fall Winter 2007/08 (page 159), Spring Summer 2008 (page 160), Fall Winter 2008/09 (page 161)
www.lindaloudermilk.com

Linda Loudermilk's environmentally friendly collections count amongst the best and most exciting in the green fashion scene. The designer's original non-eco, yet internationally successful Prêt-à-Porter collection did not truly satisfy her. "I created beauty, but beauty without soul." She set out to change this and started getting involved in ethically correct apparel. Soon she introduced the term "luxury eco" for her fashion. All her collections today are made of sustainable, yet very exclusive materials developed and researched by Linda Loudermilk, a variety of scientists and different producers from all over the world. Manufacturing takes place mainly in the USA and each of her pieces is perfected by hand. Linda Loudermilk was the first fashion designer to successfully combine ecological and luxury aspects: her collections are available in luxury stores throughout the world, such as New York's Bergdorf Goodman. Her fashion imbues the eco term "sustainability" with innovative and fresh overtones.

Die umweltfreundlichen Kollektionen von Linda Loudermilk zählen zu den hochwertigsten und aufregendsten in der grünen Modeszene. Die Designerin war mit einer Prêt-à-Porter Kollektion, die nicht ökologisch gerecht war, schon vor Jahren bis hin nach Paris erfolgreich, aber dabei selbst nicht glücklich. „Ich kreierte Schönheit, aber Schönheit ohne Seele". Das wollte sie ändern und begann über ethisch korrekte Kleidung nachzudenken. Schon bald darauf führte sie für ihre Mode den Begriff „Luxury Eco" ein. Alle ihre Kollektionen bestehen heute aus nachhaltigen und besonders exklusiven Materialien, die Linda Loudermilk auf der ganzen Welt mit verschiedensten Wissenschaftlern und Herstellern entwickelte und recherchierte. Heute werden sie zum größten Teil in den USA hergestellt und mit Handarbeit vollendet. Linda Loudermilk war die erste Modedesignerin, die den Luxus- und Ökoaspekt zusammenbrachte. Und das mit Erfolg: Ihre Kollektionen werden weltweit in Luxuskaufhäusern wie zum Beispiel Bergdorf Goodman in New York angeboten. Ihre Mode verleiht dem Öko-Begriff „Nachhaltigkeit" einen innovativen und frischen Beiklang.

Patrick Lafrontière

Fall Winter 2008/09
www.patrick-lafrontiere.com

The designer Patrick Lafrontière from French-Guyana creates wearable works of art from natural materials such as palm leaves, coconut fiber, straw, or bast—basically everything he comes across in the subtropical north of South America. His fashion is innovative eco couture, which he exhibits on the international stage such as the "Ethical Fashion Show" in Paris. His unique hand-fashioned pieces are thoroughly innovative and mostly end up in museums, or in the hands of enthusiasts or collectors, rather than in commercial boutiques. Patrick Lafrontière is not only a creator of fashion but also an artist and philosopher. He sees himself as a natural living creature that adapts itself and its work to the natural cycle of life. He uses materials provided by nature to create imaginative clothing, which in turn makes its wearer a part of nature.

Der Designer Patrick Lafrontière aus Französisch-Guyana kreiert tragbare Kunstwerke aus rein natürlichen Materialien. Er verwendet pflanzliche Rohstoffe wie z.B. Palmblätter, Kokosfasern, Stroh oder Bast, die er in seiner subtropischen Heimat im Norden Südamerikas vorfindet. Seine Mode ist innovative Eco-Couture, die er nicht nur in Südamerika, sondern auch international, unter anderem in Paris auf der Messe „Ethical Fashion Show", präsentiert. Die von ihm selbst handgefertigten Unikate sind eine Innovation und landen eher als Installationen in Museen, bei Liebhabern oder Sammlern als in kommerziellen Modeboutiquen. Patrick Lafrontière ist nicht nur Modeschöpfer, sondern vielmehr Künstler und Philosoph. Er sieht sich als Lebewesen in der Natur, das sich und seine Arbeit ihrem natürlichen Kreislauf einfügt. Die von ihr gegebenen Materialien verwandelt er in fantasievolle Kleider, die seine Träger wiederum zu einem Teil der Natur machen.

Eco-glossary

Ethical-Trade

The aim of ethical trade, in other words ethically and socially responsible trade, is to secure the rights of workers in the whole production chain from producing the materials to apparel manufacturing. Ethical trade directly supports small producers from developing countries.

Fair-Trade

Global trade provides the original producer, third world farmers, not even with the basics, especially in the case of agricultural products such as cotton. Middlemen take the largest share of the profits—the reason why conventional trade is deemed to be "unfair". The term „Fair-Trade" speaks for itself. This concept, on the other hand, specifically supports disadvantaged small farmers in developing countries. It aims to guarantee a minimum price above world market rates for sustainable raw materials such as cotton, which covers both living and production costs. This is achieved through long term delivery contracts and contacts, direct trade with producers without middlemen or prefinancing, while adhering to ecological standards. Organizations belonging to the "Fair-Trade" labeling organization (FLO) award an internationally valid fair trade certificate for the fulfillment of these criteria. Other awards include the "International Fair-Trade Association" (IFAT) which supports fair trade with its 300 organizations in over 70 countries. The international certification organization FLO-CERT checks regularly on producers, traders, and licensees to guarantee adherence to Fair-Trade standards.

Certification

Certification is a system that sets standards and checks adherence to these standards for products, manufacturing techniques, and trade contacts. Apparel thus certified is guaranteed to adhere to these standards. Certificates are awarded for a period of time, and firms are independently monitored in view of those standards. Manufacturers understand the certificate as a decision-making aid for consumers, a recognized stamp of quality of their products and an advertisement. Textile certification serves to prove adherence to environmental and social standards, as is the case for third world products. They guarantee better conditions for local producers according to Fair-Trade criteria (see above). Certification programs vary depending on regional differences, but all adhere to the basic concepts—they are autonomous. Successful certification depends on fulfillment of criteria such as prohibition of child labor, forced labor, discrimination, guarantee of wages which one can live on, and humane working conditions.

Some of the certification systems for textiles mentioned in this book:

Control Union, previously Skal International, is the world's leading control and certification institute for sustainable manufacturing and products. Control Union certificates are recognized by regulators of nearly all countries. Control Union offers two certification programs for sustainable textile production: "EKO Sustainable Textile" which follows GOTS guidelines ("Global Organic Textile" standard) and "Organic Exchange".

Nordic Ecolabel is a conglomeration of Danish, Finish, Icelandic, Norwegian, and Swedish certification institutions. The certificate's logo is a swan.

"Ecocert" is a French certification program.

The "International Community for Research and Testing of Textile Ecology" (**Eco-Tex**) grants the "Confidence in Textiles" certificate. It boasts 17 testing institutes in Europe and Japan and is represented in more than 40 countries. The system tests for chemicals and bleaching agents with adverse health effects.

EU Eco Label

The EU environmental certificate helps consumers identify environmentally friendly products and services. All products marked with the "flower" have been subject to strict ecological and usage criteria.

SA 8000 (Standard for Social Accountability):

The SA 8000 standard helps differentiate those products produced in environmentally friendly and socially fair circumstances from companies which display a total disregard of the environment, as well as working and living conditions of their workforce. The SA 8000 standard regulates social standards for companies and ensures social responsibility to employees. SA 8000 certifies workshops and factories.

ISO certified

ISO 9001 is an international standard for quality and transparency at all levels. ISO certification enables organic cotton to be treated in a separate process without mixing it, something which is demanded by eco certification. World-wide there is an ever increasing number of certification institutes controlling organic cotton farming.

Eco Cotton Certification

Cotton covers half of the global textile market. It is an important source of income for millions of small scale

Eco-glossary

farmers, especially in developing countries. Conventional cotton is very susceptible to pests. As a result large amounts of highly toxic pesticides and other dangerous chemicals are applied with serious consequences for both health and the environment.

Organic cotton is grown in controlled ecological farming systems according to clearly defined standards. Controlled organic farming prohibits the use of toxic pesticides and fertilizers as well as the usage of genetically modified organisms. Controlled organic farming aims at strengthening biologically diverse systems, regenerating soil fertility, and creating a healthy environment.

World-wide there is an ever increasing number of certification institutes controlling organic cotton farming.

Organic Cotton

Cotton covers half of the global textile market. It is an important source of income for millions of small scale farmers, especially in developing countries. Conventional cotton is very susceptible to pests. As a result large amounts of highly toxic pesticides and other dangerous chemicals are applied with serious consequences for both health and the environment. Organic cotton farming prohibits the usage of toxic pesticides, herbicides, or insecticides as well as genetically modified organisms. The result is an organic product. The plants must not—as is commonplace in normal industrial farming—be defoliated for the harvest, and the cotton must be picked by hand. These measures contribute to the up to 40 percent higher costs compared to conventionally farmed cotton. The term "organic" describes an eco system's natural nutrient cycle and its ability of self-regulation. Organic farming is subject to strict legal guidelines and minimum standards.

Sustainability

The concept of sustainability describes the usage of a naturally regenerating system which preserves its basic properties and whose crop can re-grow naturally. Organically grown cotton is one of these crops.

For some years now the term sustainability has come to be a maxim for humankind's future development as well as a solution to environmental problems. "Sustainable development" is both environmentally and ecologically sound—for eons to come. Sustainability is the permanent unison of environmental, economical, and social dimensions. A sustainable policy's core points include protection of the environment and nature without creating social tensions, employment through ecological and social modernization, implementation of social and environmental standards throughout the world, industrial democracy, and the improvement of working and living conditions.

Recycling

Recycling describes the environmentally friendly re-usage of old materials, vintage apparel, surplus or waste materials from production processes. They can be used as raw materials for new designs. Frequently, designers create new apparel out of old or transform them into new pieces of clothing. No two recycled items of clothing are alike which makes for highly individual hand-made pieces.

Öko-Glossar

Ethical Trade

Ethical Trade, sprich ethisch und sozial korrekter Handel hat es zum Ziel, die Rechte der Arbeiter in der ganzen Produktionskette der Modeindustrie, von der Herstellung der Materialien bis zur Produktion der Kleidung, zu sichern. Fair Trade fördert direkt die Kleinproduzenten in den Entwicklungsländern.

Fair-Trade

Fair-Trade steht für fairen Handel. Der globalisierte Handel bringt dem ursprünglichen Produzenten, den Bauern der Dritten Welt, vor allem bei Agrarprodukten wie z.B. Baumwolle, nicht einmal das Existenzminimum ein. Besonders der Zwischenhandel streicht einen großen Teil des Endpreises aus. Daher wird der konventionelle Handel als „unfair" eingeschätzt. Dagegen fördert das Konzept des „Fairen Handels" gezielt die stark benachteiligten Kleinbauern in den Entwicklungsländern. Er will ihnen durch nachwachsende Rohstoffe wie z.B. Baumwolle einen Mindestpreis über dem Niveau der Weltmarktpreise, die die Lebenshaltungs- und Produktionskosten deckt, garantieren. Das soll u.a. durch langfristige Lieferverträge und -beziehungen, direkten Handel mit den Produzentengruppen ohne Zwischenhändler, Vorfinanzierung sowie der Einhaltung ökologischer Standards, erreicht werden. Bei Erfüllung dieser Kriterien verleihen Organisationen, die im Verband „Fairtrade Labelling Organizations International" (FLO) zusammengeschlossen sind, ein international einheitliches Fair-Trade Siegel. Daneben gibt es andere Siegel wie z.B. das des Verbandes „International Fair Trade Association" (IFAT), der mit 300 Fair-Trade Organisationen in 70 Ländern weltweit den Fairen-Handel fördert. Um die Einhaltung von Fair-Trade Kriterien sicher zustellen, kontrolliert die internationale Zertifizierungsstelle

FLO-CERT regelmäßig Produzentengruppen, Händler und Lizenznehmer.

Zertifizierung

Die Zertifizierung ist ein System, das Standards setzt und mit dessen Hilfe die Einhaltung dieser Standards für Produkte, ihre Herstellungsverfahren und Handelsbeziehungen nachgewiesen werden können. Die mit einem Etikett, dem Zertifikat, versehenen Textilprodukte garantieren den Verbrauchern die Einhaltung der Standards. Die Zertifikate werden oft zeitlich befristet vergeben und hinsichtlich der Standards unabhängig kontrolliert. Das Zertifikat wird von Herstellern als Entscheidungshilfe für den Verbraucher und als Mittel zur Qualitätssicherung ihrer Produkte angesehen und dient außerdem der Werbung.

Die textilen Zertifizierungen dienen zum Nachweis der Einhaltung von Umwelt- und Sozialstandards, z.B. bei der Zertifizierung von Produkten aus Entwicklungsländern. Sie garantieren bessere Konditionen für die dortigen Produzenten nach Fair-Trade-Kriterien (siehe oben). Zertifizierungsprogramme variieren in Abhängigkeit von regionalen Unterschieden, unterliegen jedoch bestimmten Grundkonzepten, sie sind autonom. Kriterien, wie dem Verbot von Kinder- und Zwangsarbeit, Diskriminierung, Garantie von Existenz sichernden Löhnen, menschenwürdigen Arbeitsbedingungen sollten grundsätzlich eingehalten worden sein, um ein Zertifikat verliehen zu bekommen.

Hier einige der in diesem Buch erwähnten Zertifizierungssysteme für Textilien:

Control Union, zuvor Skal International, ist die weltweit führende Prüfungs- und Zertifizierungsstelle für nachhaltige Produktion und Produkte. Die Zertifikate von

Control Union werden von den Behörden fast aller Länder anerkannt. Sie bietet zwei Zertifizierungsprogramme bzgl. nachhaltiger textiler Produktion: „EKO Sustainable Textile" nach GOTS (dem „Global Organic Textile" Standard) und „Organic Exchange".

Nordic Ecolabel ist ein Zusammenschluss verschiedener Zertifizierungsstellen der Länder Dänemark, Finnland, Island, Norwegen und Schweden. Das Logo auf dem Zertifikat ist ein Schwan.

„Ecocert" ist ein Zertifizierungsprogramm aus Frankreich

Den Öko-Tex Standard 100% engl: „Confidence in Textiles" vergibt die „Internationale Gemeinschaft für Forschung und Prüfung auf dem Gebiet der Textilökologie" (Öko-Tex), die mit 17 Prüfinstituten in Europa und Japan und in mehr als 40 Ländern vertreten ist. Das Prüfsystem testet Chemikalien und Bleichmittel, welche schädliche Wirkungen auf die Gesundheit von Menschen haben. Es wird für ein Jahr ausgestellt und kann nach wiederholter erfolgreicher Prüfung verlängert werden.

EU Eco Label

Das EU-Umweltzeichen erleichtert dem europäischen Verbraucher das Erkennen umweltfreundlicher Produkte und Dienstleistungen. Alle mit der „Blume" gekennzeichneten Produkte sind auf die Einhaltung strenger ökologischer und gebrauchs-tauglichkeitsbezogener Kriterien geprüft worden.

SA 8000 (Standard for Social Accountability)

Der SA 8000 Standard dient der Unterscheidung von umweltschonend und sozial fair hergestellten Produkten im Gegensatz zu Unternehmen, welche die Umwelt

Öko-Glossar

ausbeuten und Arbeits- und Lebensbedingungen der Menschen ignorieren. Die Norm der SA 8000 reguliert Sozialstandards für Unternehmen. Dadurch wird soziale Verantwortung gegenüber den Mitarbeitern gesichert. Der SA 8000 ist für die Zertifizierung von Fabrikationsstätten verantwortlich.

ISO zertifiziert

ISO 9001 ist eine internationale Norm für Qualität der Arbeit und für Transparenz auf allen Stufen. Die ISO-Zertifizierung erlaubt es, die Bio-Baumwolle in einem separaten Durchgang zu verarbeiten, ohne dass sie gemischt wird. Das verlangt die Bio-Zertifizierung. Weltweit gibt es immer mehr Zertifizierungsorganisationen, die den ökologischen Anbau von Baumwolle kontrollieren.

Zertifizierung von Bio-Baumwolle

Baumwolle deckt die Hälfte des globalen Faserbedarfs. Sie ist eine wichtige Einkommensquelle für Millionen von Kleinbauern, v. a. in den Entwicklungsländern. Konventionelle Baumwolle ist sehr anfällig für Insekten. Daher werden große Mengen hoch toxischer Insektizide und anderer gefährlicher Chemikalien zur Baumwollproduktion eingesetzt. Diese haben ernste Folgen für Gesundheit und Umwelt. Bio-Baumwolle wird in kontrolliert biologischen Landwirtschaftssystemen nach klar festgelegten Standards angebaut. Kontrolliert biologische Landwirtschaft verbietet die Nutzung von toxischen Pestiziden und Düngemitteln sowie die Verwendung gentechnisch veränderter Organismen. Der kontrolliert biologische Anbau strebt danach, biologisch diverse landwirtschaftliche Systeme aufzubauen, die Bodenfruchtbarkeit zu regenerieren, aufrechtzuerhalten und eine gesunde Umwelt zu fördern. Weltweit gibt es immer mehr Zertifizierungsorganisationen, die den ökologischen Anbau von Baumwolle kontrollieren.

Organische Baumwolle

Baumwolle deckt die Hälfte des globalen Faserbedarfs. Sie ist eine wichtige Einkommensquelle für Millionen von Kleinbauern, v.a. in den Entwicklungsländern. Konventionelle Baumwolle ist sehr anfällig für Insekten. Daher werden große Mengen gefährlicher Chemikalien zur Baumwollproduktion eingesetzt. Diese haben ernste Folgen für Gesundheit und Umwelt. Beim ökologischen Anbau von Baumwolle wird auf die Verwendung von toxischen Pflanzenspritzmitteln, Pestiziden, Herbiziden oder Insektiziden und auch auf den Einsatz gentechnisch veränderter Organismen verzichtet. Dabei entstehen rein biologische Produkte. Die Pflanzen dürfen nicht - wie bei industriellem Anbau sonst üblich - zum Ernten entlaubt werden. Die Baumwollbälle müssen von Hand gepflückt werden. Diese Maßnahmen machen Bio-Baumwolle um bis zu 40% teurer als konventionell angebaute Fasern. Der Begriff „organic" beschreibt den natürlichen Nährstoffkreislauf eines Ökosystems und seine Fähigkeit, sich selbst regulieren zu können. Ein organischer Anbau unterliegt strengen gesetzlichen Richtlinien und Mindeststandards.

Nachhaltigkeit

Das Konzept der Nachhaltigkeit beschreibt die Nutzung eines regenerierbaren natürlichen Systems, das in seinen wesentlichen Eigenschaften erhalten bleibt und sein Bestand auf natürliche Weise nachwachsen kann. Dazu gehört z.B. der Anbau organischer Baumwolle. Der Begriff der Nachhaltigkeit gilt seit einigen Jahren als Leitfaden für eine zukunftsfähige Entwicklung der Menschheit und als Lösung von Umweltproblemen. Eine „nachhaltige Entwicklung" ist dauerhaft umweltgerecht, ökologisch-dauerhaft und zukunftsverträglich. Nachhaltigkeit ist die dauerhafte Einheit von ökologischen, ökonomischen und sozialen Dimensionen. Zu den Kern-

punkten einer Nachhaltigkeitspolitik gehören der Schutz von Umwelt und Natur ohne soziale Verwerfungen, die Beschäftigungssicherung durch ökologische und soziale Modernisierung, die Durchsetzung von Sozial- und Umweltmindeststandards weltweit, die Demokratisierung der Arbeitswelt und auch die Verbesserung der Arbeits- und Lebensbedingungen.

Recycling

Recyceln beschreibt die umweltfreundliche Wiederverwertung von alten Materialien, Vintage-Kleidung, Produktionsresten oder -überschüssen. Sie können als Rohstoff für neue Entwürfe verwendet werden. Oft wandeln die Designer alte Textilien um oder transformieren sie zu neuen Modellen. Kein recyceltes Bekleidungsstück gleicht dem anderen. Dadurch entstehen handgemachte Unikate, die sehr individuell sind.

imprint

Bibliographic information published by the Deutsche Nationalbibliothek
The Deutsche Nationalbibliothek lists this publication in the Deutsche Nationalbibliografie; detailed bibliographic data are available in the Internet at http://dnb.d-nb.de.

ISBN: 978-3-89986-103-7

© 2008 avedition GmbH, Ludwigsburg
© 2008 Edited and produced by
fusion publishing GmbH, Stuttgart . Los Angeles

Printed in Austria
by Vorarlberger Verlagsanstalt AG, Dornbirn

Paper: EuroBulk by M-real Hallein AG
It is PEFC, DIN EN ISO 9001, DIN EN ISO 14001 and EMAS certified.

avedition GmbH
Königsallee 57 | 71638 Ludwigsburg | Germany
p +49-7141-1477391 | f +49-7141-1477399
www.avedition.com | contact@avedition.com

Team: Christine Anna Bierhals (Author),
Katharina Feuer (Editorial management), Claudia Maier (Layout), Jan Hausberg (Imaging & prepress),
Zoratti studio editoriale, Wingertsberg (Translations)

Cover: Leila Hafzi, Emile Ashley/Ashley Studio, stylist: Hege Jeanette Bakken, model: Linn Rafdal
Backcover: Photographs by Eric Guillemain for Environmental Justice Foundation's Cotton Campaign

Christine Anna Bierhals
Born in Germany in 1980. Studied fashion design and journalism. Currently works as a fashion journalist and as stylist for advertising and fashion.

Christine Anna Bierhals
1980 in Deutschland geboren. Studierte Modedesign und Journalismus. Heute als Modejournalistin und als Stylistin in der Werbe- und Modebranche tätig.

green designed series:

green designed: Kitchen & Dining
green designed: Future Cars

Further information and links at
www.bestdesigned.com
www.fusion-publishing.com

All books are released in
German and English

Special thanks to
Besonderen Dank an
www.lohas.de